LIFE SKILLS FOR TEENAGE BOYS

HOW TO MANAGE MONEY, BE CONFIDENT, MAKE FRIENDS, COMMUNICATE, DEVELOP RELATIONSHIPS, SET GOALS, COOK, CLEAN, AND BECOME AN INDEPENDENT YOUNG ADULT

GRACE DANIELS

CONTENTS

ALSO BY GRACE DANIELS

Life Skills for Kids

Life Skills for Teenage Girls

The Growth Mindset for Kids

The Growth Mindset for Teens

Career Planning for Teens

Social Skills for Teens

Building Confident, Brave and Beautiful Girls

Inspiring Stories for Confident, Brave and Beautiful Girls

Inspiring Stories for Kind, Confident and Brave Boys

INTRODUCTION
WHY ARE LIFE SKILLS SO IMPORTANT?

As you venture into the exciting and challenging world of teenagehood, developing the skills you need to thrive and succeed is essential. But don't worry because this book is here to help you acquire the life skills that will enable you to overcome obstacles, achieve your goals, and live your best life.

At this stage in your life, it's crucial to develop both practical and emotional skills that will set you up for success in all aspects of your life. Whether managing your time wisely, communicating effectively, making sound financial decisions, or solving problems creatively, mastering these skills will give you the confidence and tools you need to thrive.

Learning new things can sometimes be daunting, so this book was created to make acquiring life skills fun, engaging, and interactive. You'll find a ton of exciting activities, information, and tips to apply these skills to your daily life.

Throughout this book, we'll encourage you to step outside your comfort zone, take calculated risks, and embrace new challenges. We believe in you and your potential to accomplish amazing things. So, let's embark on this journey together and discover the power of life skills!

CHAPTER 1
A GUIDE TO CONFIDENCE AND SELF-AWARENESS

Confidence and self-awareness are two traits that can make all the difference when it comes to achieving your goals and living a fulfilling life. Confidence just means that you believe in yourself and your abilities. When you're confident, you're not afraid to take risks or try new things. You trust yourself to make the right decisions and handle any challenges that come your way. Self-awareness, on the other hand, is the ability to recognize your own thoughts, feelings, and behaviors. It involves understanding your strengths and weaknesses, as well as how you interact with others and the world around you.

Both confidence and self-awareness are essential for personal growth and success. When you're confident and self-aware, you're more likely to pursue your goals with determination and resilience (and stand right back up when you get knocked down). You're also more likely to develop strong relationships with others and be able to communicate effectively.

The relationship between confidence and self-awareness is a bit of a chicken-and-egg situation. When you're confident, you're more likely to be self-aware because you're not afraid to examine yourself honestly and acknowledge both your strengths and weaknesses. At the same time, when you're self-aware, you're more likely to be confident because you know your own abilities and are able to use them effectively.

However, it's critical to understand the difference between confidence and cockiness. Confidence comes from a place of self-assuredness, while cockiness comes from a misplaced feeling of superiority. Confident people acknowledge their strengths and weaknesses and are open to feedback, while cocky people believe they're always right and don't listen to others. Work to strike a balance between confidence and humility, recognizing your own worth without putting others down.

TIPS TO BUILD SELF-AWARENESS

Self-awareness can help you build better relationships. When you understand your own thoughts and feelings, you are better able to understand the thoughts and feelings of others. This can help you communicate more effectively, build stronger friendships, and be a better listener. Below are a few ways you can learn how to practice self-awareness (Morin 2021):

Take time for reflection: One of the best ways to build self-awareness is to take time for reflection. This means setting aside a few minutes each day to think about your thoughts, feelings, and actions. You can do this in many ways, such as through meditation, journaling, expressing yourself with passions (such as writing, exercising, or other arts) or even sitting quietly and thinking.

For example, you might take a few minutes each evening to reflect on your day. Ask yourself questions like, "What did I do well today?" and "What could I have done better?" This can help you become more aware of your strengths and weaknesses and give you a better understanding of yourself.

Ask for feedback: It can be hard to see ourselves clearly, so it can be helpful to ask others for feedback. This might mean asking your friends, family, or a trusted teacher or coach for their honest opinion on your strengths and weaknesses. Be open to constructive criticism and use it as an opportunity to grow.

For example, you might ask your friend who is great at sports to watch you play and give you feedback on your technique. Or, you might ask your teacher for feedback on your essay to see how you can improve your writing skills.

Practice mindfulness: Mindfulness is the practice of being present in the moment and paying attention to your thoughts and feelings without judgment. By practicing mindfulness regularly, you can learn to be more aware of your thoughts and feelings in the present moment.

For example, you might practice mindfulness by taking a few deep breaths and focusing on your senses. What do you hear? What do you smell? What do you feel? By doing this, you can become more aware of your surroundings and your own thoughts and feelings.

Try new things: Stepping outside your comfort zone and trying new things can be a great way to learn more about yourself. By pushing yourself, you can discover your strengths and weaknesses and gain a better understanding of what you're capable of.

For example, you might try a new sport or hobby that you've always been interested in but have never tried. Or, you might take on a new challenge at school, like joining the debate team or trying out for the school play. By trying new things, you can gain new experiences and insights into yourself.

TIPS TO BE MORE CONFIDENT

It's important to understand that confidence is a crucial component of success and well-being in many different areas of life. Here are some reasons why building confidence is so important (Lyness 2018):

Improved decision-making skills: Confidence gives you a sense of control over your life and your decisions. When you are more sure of your beliefs and position, you will be able to make decisions quicker and from a more informed perspective.

Better relationships: Confidence can help you build stronger relationships with others. When you're confident, you're more likely to be assertive, communicate clearly, and set boundaries. This can make it easier for others to understand and respect you.

More success: Confidence is often linked to success. When you're confident in your abilities, you're more likely to take risks, pursue opportunities, and achieve your goals.

Increased resilience: Confidence can help you bounce back from setbacks and failures. When you're confident in your abilities, you're more likely to keep trying, even when things get tough.

Overall, building confidence is an important part of becoming a successful and well-adjusted adult. Remember that confidence is something that can be developed over time, so don't be afraid to take risks and try new things to help boost your self-esteem.

Here are a few ways you can work to increase your confidence (Lyness 2018):

Focus on what you're good at: Take some time to identify your strengths, and find ways to use them in your daily life. Whether it's playing sports, being creative, or excelling in academics, use your strengths to your advantage and feel proud of what you can do.

Practice self-care: Taking care of your physical and mental health is an important part of building confidence. Make sure to get enough sleep, exercise regularly, and eat healthy foods. Taking care of your body can make you feel better about yourself and give you more energy to tackle the day. Also, take some time to do things that make you happy and relaxed, such as playing video games, listening to music, or hanging out with friends.

Set goals: Having goals to work toward can give you a sense of purpose and direction. Set realistic goals for yourself and work toward achieving them. Start with small goals and work your way up to bigger ones. Celebrate your accomplishments along the way, and don't get discouraged if you face setbacks. Keep pushing yourself toward your goals, and your confidence will grow as you see your progress.

Get out of your comfort zone: Trying new things can be scary, but it's a great way to build confidence. Challenge yourself to try something outside of your comfort zone, such as joining a new club, trying a new sport, or volunteering for a cause you care about. Even if you don't succeed at first, the experience will help you grow and learn, and you'll feel more confident after having tried.

Surround yourself with positive people: The people you spend time with can have a big impact on your confidence. Surround yourself with friends and family who support and encourage you. Avoid negative influences and people who bring you down. Remember, you deserve to be around people who lift you up and make you feel good about yourself.

WAYS TO PRACTICE BUILDING CONFIDENCE AND SELF-AWARENESS *DAILY*

It's time to talk about a few different activities and practices you can do *daily* to increase your confidence and self-awareness:

- Exercise: Regular exercise improves self-confidence and self-awareness. Try incorporating some form of physical activity into your daily routine, whether running, lifting weights, or playing sports. Aim for at least 30 minutes of exercise per day.
- Practice public speaking: Speaking in front of others can be nerve-wracking, but it's also a great way to build confidence. Try to find opportunities to practice public speaking, such as giving a presentation in class or participating in a debate club.
- Volunteer: Helping others can be a great way to build self-confidence and gain a sense of purpose. Look for volunteer opportunities in your community, such as helping out at a food bank or animal shelter.
- Learn a new skill: Trying new things can help you gain a sense of accomplishment and self-worth. Consider learning a new skill, such as playing an instrument, coding, or cooking.
- Mindfulness meditation: Practicing mindfulness meditation can help you become more aware of your thoughts and emotions, and develop greater self-awareness. Find a quiet place to sit, close your eyes, and focus on your breath. When your mind wanders, gently bring your attention back to your breath.
- Creative expression: Engaging in creative activities such as writing, drawing, or playing music can help you express your emotions and gain a sense of accomplishment. Try setting aside time each day to engage in a creative activity that you enjoy.
- Socializing: Spending time with friends and family can help you build social skills and develop confidence in social situations. Make an effort to connect with others and participate in social activities.
- Reading: Reading can help you gain knowledge and insights that can improve your confidence and self-awareness. Try reading books on topics that interest you, or self-help books that focus on personal growth and development.

It's important to understand that developing confidence and self-awareness is crucial in navigating the challenges of adolescence and preparing for adulthood. By building a strong sense of self and believing in your abilities, you can overcome obstacles, form healthy relationships, and pursue your goals with conviction. Remember, having confidence doesn't mean you have to be perfect, but rather acknowledging your strengths and weaknesses and taking risks to grow and learn.

As you continue on your personal development journey, it's also important to focus on emotional intelligence, which we'll be covering in the next chapter. Emotional intelligence involves understanding and managing your own emotions, as well as recognizing and empathizing with the emotions of others. This skill will help you communicate effectively, build stronger connections, and handle conflicts with maturity and empathy. By combining confidence, self-awareness, and emotional intelligence, you can become a well-rounded and capable young adult.

CHAPTER 2
WHAT IS EMOTIONAL INTELLIGENCE?

Emotional intelligence is the ability to understand and manage your own emotions, as well as recognize and respond to the emotions of others. It involves being aware of your own feelings and the feelings of others and using that awareness to guide your thoughts, actions, and interactions with others.

But why is this even an important skill for you to learn? Well, here are a few different reasons (The University of Queensland 2023):

Building positive relationships: Having emotional intelligence is essential for building positive relationships with others. By being aware of your own emotions and those of others, you can communicate more effectively, resolve conflicts more easily, and build stronger connections with those around you.

Succeeding academically and professionally: Developing emotional intelligence can also help you succeed academically and professionally. It can help you manage stress, stay motivated, and work effectively with others in group projects or when collaborating on assignments.

Achieving personal goals: Emotional intelligence is an important factor when it comes to achieving your personal goals. By understanding your own motivations and feelings, you can work toward your goals more effectively and with a greater sense of purpose.

Remember, emotional intelligence is a skill that can be learned and developed over time. By practicing self-awareness and empathy, you can improve your emotional intelligence and become a more effective communicator and leader in all aspects of your life.

HOW TO BUILD SELF-MANAGEMENT SKILLS

Self-management skills refer to your ability to manage your own thoughts, feelings, and behaviors in a way that helps you achieve your goals and lead a fulfilling life. These skills include things like time management, goal-setting, emotional regulation, and self-discipline.

In other words, self-management skills are all about being able to control your own actions, even when faced with difficult situations or distractions. It's about having the ability to set priorities, plan and execute tasks, and stay focused on your goals, even when things get tough.

Developing self-management skills is essential and can help you make better decisions, achieve your goals, and lead a more fulfilling life. Here are some effective strategies to build self-management skills:

Visualize success: Visualization is a powerful tool that can help you stay focused on your goals and build self-discipline. Take a few minutes each day to visualize yourself successfully achieving your goals. See yourself taking the necessary steps to achieve your goals and overcoming any obstacles that come your way.

Practice positive self-talk: Self-talk is the internal dialogue that you have with yourself. It can be positive or negative, and it can have a huge impact on your emotions and actions. Practice positive self-talk by using affirmations such as "I can do this," or "I am capable of achieving my goals."

Deep breathing: Deep breathing is a simple yet effective way to manage your emotions and stay calm in stressful situations. Take a few deep breaths when you feel overwhelmed or anxious. Focus on your breath and let go of any negative thoughts.

Prioritize your time: Time management is a crucial aspect of self-management. Make a schedule and prioritize your time to ensure that you are focusing on the most important tasks first. Avoid procrastination by setting deadlines and sticking to them.

By developing self-management skills, you can improve your decision-making skills, achieve your goals, and lead a more fulfilling life. Remember to practice visualization, positive self-talk, deep breathing, and prioritize your time. With practice and patience, you can become more self-disciplined and successful in all areas of your life.

WHAT IS SOCIAL AWARENESS?

Social awareness is all about understanding the world around us and the people in it. It means being aware of the different cultures, beliefs, and experiences that exist in society, and how they can affect people's thoughts, feelings, and behaviors.

Social awareness also involves being able to recognize and understand the emotions of others. This might mean recognizing when a friend is feeling upset or stressed, and knowing how to offer them support and comfort. Or, it might mean being mindful of the impact that our actions and words can have on others and making an effort to treat people with kindness and respect.

Here are a few other ways practicing social awareness can help you develop emotional intelligence (Young, 2020):

It helps you understand your own emotions. When you are aware of the emotions of those around you, it can help you better understand your own emotions. You may start to recognize patterns in your own emotional reactions and be better equipped to manage them in the future.

It improves your communication skills. When you are socially aware, you are better able to communicate with others in a way that is respectful and empathetic. You are able to pick up on social cues and adjust your communication style accordingly, which can help avoid misunderstandings and improve relationships.

It improves your ability to work in a team. In many situations, working in a team is necessary to achieve a common goal. When you have social awareness, you are better able to work with others in a way that is respectful and productive. You are able to recognize the strengths and weaknesses of your team members and adjust your approach accordingly.

Overall, social awareness is an important skill to have, as it can help us to navigate the complex social world we live in and build stronger, more positive relationships with the people around us.

Here are a few tips for building your social awareness skills :

Observe body language: People's body language can tell you a lot about how they're feeling. Pay attention to things like facial expressions, posture, and tone of voice to get a better understanding of someone's emotions.

Read books or watch documentaries about different cultures: Learning about other cultures can help you develop empathy and understanding for people who may be different from you.

Volunteer in your community: Volunteering can expose you to different people and experiences, and help you develop a greater sense of compassion and empathy for others.

Seek out diverse social groups: Surrounding yourself with people who come from different backgrounds or have different experiences can help you broaden your perspective and develop a greater sense of empathy.

Use social media mindfully: Social media can be a great tool for connecting with others, but it can also be a source of misinformation and negativity. Use social media mindfully by fact-checking information, avoiding engaging in negative conversations, and promoting positivity.

RELATIONSHIP MANAGEMENT SKILLS—WHAT ARE THEY?

Relationship management skills are essential to building strong and healthy relationships with the people in your life, whether they are friends, family members, or romantic partners. These skills involve the ability to communicate effectively, resolve conflicts, and work cooperatively with others. You have already discovered self-management skills and social awareness skills, and these will really help you with this next skill!

They all work together to help you be more emotionally intelligent and aware. To be successful at relationship management, you need to be able to do the following:

Communicate clearly and effectively: Good communication is key to building healthy relationships. You need to be able to express your thoughts and feelings clearly and listen in a way that shows respect for the other person's perspective.

Resolve conflicts: Conflicts are a natural part of any relationship, but it's important to know how to handle them in a constructive way. This involves finding common ground, compromising when necessary, and working toward a mutually beneficial solution.

Work cooperatively with others: Whether you're part of a team or in a one-on-one relationship, you need to be able to work effectively with others. This means being open-minded, flexible, and respectful of other people's opinions and ideas.

Self-management and social awareness skills are going to be very important components of relationship management, but here are a few additional skills that you should focus on to improve your ability to manage your relationships effectively (Young, 2020):

Assertiveness: Being assertive means standing up for yourself in a way that is respectful and clear. It's important to be able to express your needs and boundaries while also being open to compromise.

Forgiveness: Forgiveness is essential for maintaining healthy relationships over the long term. It involves letting go of grudges and resentment and being willing to move forward in a positive way.

Adaptability: Being able to adapt to different situations and personalities is important for managing connections effectively. This involves being flexible, open-minded, and willing to compromise when necessary.

PRACTICES FOR BUILDING EMOTIONAL INTELLIGENCE SKILLS *DAILY*

- Writing: Take a few minutes each day to write down your thoughts and feelings wherever you want. This will help you become more aware of your emotions and provide an outlet for processing them. You can start by setting aside a few minutes every day to write in a journal. You can write about anything that comes to mind—how you're feeling, what's going on in your life, or even just random thoughts. Don't worry about grammar or spelling, just let your thoughts flow onto the page.

- Mindful Breathing: Practicing mindfulness can help you regulate your emotions and reduce stress. One way to do this is through mindful breathing. You can start by finding a quiet place where you won't be disturbed. Sit comfortably and close your eyes. Take a deep breath in through your nose, hold it for a few seconds, and then exhale slowly through your mouth. Repeat this for a few minutes, focusing on your breath and letting go of any thoughts that come to mind.
- Random Acts of Kindness: Doing something kind for someone else can boost your mood and help you build empathy and compassion. Each day, try to do one kind thing for someone else. It could be as simple as holding the door open for someone, complimenting a friend, or helping someone with a task. Notice how it makes you feel and how it affects the other person.
- Positive Affirmations: Affirmations are positive statements that can help you build confidence and self-esteem. Choose a few positive affirmations that resonate with you, such as "I am capable of achieving my goals," or "I am worthy of love and respect." Repeat them to yourself each day, either in the morning or before bed.
- Mindful Listening: Practicing mindful listening can help you communicate more effectively and build stronger relationships. When talking to someone, give them your full attention. Avoid distractions like your phone or TV. Show them that you are listening by asking questions and clarifying what they're saying. Notice your own reactions and emotions as you listen.

By incorporating these daily practices into your routine, you can improve your emotional intelligence skills in a fun and engaging way. Give them a try and see how they work for you! Emotional intelligence can help you understand and manage your own feelings and those of others, leading to better communication and stronger bonds and connections.

In the next chapter, we're going to focus on some social and communication skills that will help you develop even more social awareness. We'll cover everything from how to hold a conversation with an adult to the best social skill everyone should learn. You will discover how to communicate your thoughts in a healthy and effective way as well. Let's dive right in!

CHAPTER 3
A GUIDE TO SOCIAL AND COMMUNICATION SKILLS

You might not really see how social and communication skills are important for your future, but they play a crucial role in building positive relationships, succeeding academically, and ultimately achieving professional success.

Let's start with relationships. Having good social skills can help you make friends, form healthy romantic connections, and even improve your family connections. When you can communicate effectively, you can express your thoughts and feelings clearly, listen to what they have to say, and solve problems together. These skills can also help you navigate difficult situations, like conflicts or misunderstandings, with ease.

Now, let's talk about academics and career success. As you get older, you'll need to work with others to complete projects, collaborate on assignments, and network with professionals. Strong communication skills will help you express your ideas effectively, work well with others, and present yourself professionally. When you're able to communicate your thoughts clearly, you'll also be better able to learn from others and understand complex topics.

COMMON STRUGGLES AND HOW TO OVERCOME THEM

You might think that social skills and communication skills come naturally to some people, and that you're just not one of them. But the truth is, anyone can learn these skills with practice and effort. Some people might struggle with social skills and communication skills due to shyness, anxiety, or a lack of experience. With practice, you can build your confidence and become more comfortable in social situations. Below are a few common things teen boys struggle with when it comes to social and communication skills and how you can improve (Raus 2022):

Shyness or social anxiety: If you're feeling nervous or uncomfortable in social situations, it can be hard to know what to say or how to act. The good news is that there are plenty of ways to overcome shyness or social anxiety, like practicing relaxation techniques, joining a club or team, and gradually exposing yourself to social situations.

Lack of experience: If you haven't had many opportunities to practice social skills, it can be hard to know where to start. To overcome this, try seeking out new experiences and meeting new people. You might consider joining a club or volunteering for a cause you're passionate about.

Differences in communication styles: Sometimes, it can be hard to understand someone else's communication style, especially if they have different cultural or linguistic backgrounds. To overcome this, try to be patient and listen carefully to what others are saying. Ask questions if you're not sure you understand, and try to avoid making assumptions.

Difficulty reading social cues: Some teen boys struggle with understanding nonverbal cues, like body language and tone of voice. To overcome this, try practicing active listening (which we will talk about in just a second) and observing others carefully. Pay attention to facial expressions and body language to get a sense of how others are feeling.

Fear of rejection: One of the biggest fears that can hold you back from practicing social skills is the fear of rejection. This fear can make it hard to initiate conversations or reach out to new people. To overcome this, remind yourself that rejection is a natural part of life and it's not a reflection of your worth as a person. Also, try to focus on the positive outcomes of practicing social skills, like making new friends or building a professional network.

Digital communication overload: In today's digital age, it's easy to rely too heavily on texting, social media, and other forms of digital communication. While these tools can be useful, they can also make it harder to practice face-to-face communication skills. To overcome this, try to limit your screen time and focus on in-person interactions. Practice starting conversations with people you meet in person and resist the temptation to rely solely on digital communication.

Discomfort with small talk: Small talk is an important part of social interactions, but some teen boys may feel uncomfortable or awkward with it. To overcome this, try practicing asking open-ended questions and actively listening to the other person's responses. You can also practice making small talk with friends or family members in low-pressure situations, like over a meal or during a walk.

Remember, social and communication skills take time and effort to develop. Don't be discouraged if you don't see improvement right away. Keep practicing and seeking out new opportunities to interact with others, and you'll gradually become more confident and comfortable in social situations.

STEPS TO PRACTICE COMMUNICATION AND SOCIAL SKILLS *DAILY*

Let's dive right into a few different ways you can practice communication and social skills (Possing 2022):

- Active Listening: Paying attention to what others are saying and showing that you understand them. To practice this, try asking questions to clarify what someone has said or summarizing what they said in your own words.
- Eye Contact: Making and maintaining eye contact can show others that you are confident and engaged in the conversation. To practice, try looking directly at someone's eyes while you are talking to them, but be sure to also give your eyes a break from time to time by looking away briefly.
- Speaking Clearly: Speaking clearly and using proper grammar can make you easier to understand. To practice this, try recording yourself speaking and listening back to hear how you sound. You can also practice speaking more slowly to give yourself time to think about what you want to say.
- Nonverbal Communication: Using body language, facial expressions, and tone of voice to convey your thoughts and feelings. To practice,

try experimenting with different facial expressions and body language to see how they affect the way others perceive you. You can also practice using a tone of voice that matches your emotions.

- Conflict resolution: Finding a solution to a disagreement or problem that satisfies everyone involved. To practice, try brainstorming solutions to a problem with a friend or family member. You can also practice by seeking out and participating in group discussions where there may be differing opinions.
- Proper addressing: Knowing how to address someone properly is important, especially when interacting with adults or in formal settings. To practice, try addressing adults as "Mr." or "Ms." followed by their last name. In more formal settings, it's appropriate to use titles like "Doctor" or "Professor."
- Interacting with adults: Interacting with adults can be intimidating, but it's an important skill to have for success in academic and professional settings. To practice, try maintaining eye contact, listening actively, and using respectful language when speaking with adults. It's also important to be aware of cultural differences and customs when interacting with adults from different backgrounds.
- Making a good first impression: Making a good first impression is crucial in building positive relationships with others. To practice, try presenting yourself in a positive manner through your appearance, body language, and conversation. You can also practice by researching the person or organization you'll be meeting with beforehand and preparing questions or conversation topics to show your interest and engagement.
- Small talk: Engaging in casual conversation with others. To practice, try striking up a conversation with someone you don't know very well, like a classmate or coworker. You can also practice by asking open-ended questions that allow for more in-depth conversation.
- Asking questions: Showing interest in others by asking them questions. To practice, try asking someone about their hobbies, interests, or opinions on a topic. You can also practice by listening actively and responding thoughtfully to their answers.
- Active participation: Engaging in group conversations and activities. To practice, try volunteering to participate in group projects or discussions. You can also practice by contributing your ideas and opinions during group activities.

- Humor: Using appropriate humor to make others feel comfortable and laugh. To practice, try telling a joke or sharing a funny story with friends or family. You can also practice by keeping an open mind and finding humor in everyday situations.
- Gratitude: Showing appreciation for others and their contributions. To practice, try thanking someone for something they did or complimenting them on a job well done. You can also practice by expressing your gratitude through handwritten notes or other small gestures.
- Respecting boundaries: Recognizing and respecting others' personal space and emotional boundaries. To practice, try asking for permission before entering someone's personal space, like giving a hug or high-five. You can also practice by recognizing when someone may not want to talk about a certain topic and respecting their wishes.
- Patience: Taking the time to listen and understand others, even if they speak or act differently from you. To practice, try listening to someone without interrupting or judging them. You can also practice by taking a step back and considering a situation from someone else's perspective.
- Networking: Building and maintaining positive relationships with others. To practice, try attending events or joining clubs related to your interests. You can also practice by reaching out to acquaintances or professionals in your desired field for advice or mentorship.
- Open-mindedness: Being willing to consider new ideas and perspectives. To practice, try engaging in conversations with people who have different backgrounds or opinions from you. You can also practice by seeking out diverse sources of information.

Remember, these skills may take time and practice to develop, but they can benefit you in all areas of your life, including building positive relationships, succeeding academically and professionally, and even improving your own mental health and well-being. Keep an open mind and be patient with yourself as you work to improve your communication and social skills.

In the next chapter, you will discover how to handle and de-escalate conflicts, what peer pressure is and how to deal with it, and all about bullies. Improving social skills will help advance you in life and create deeper relationships; however, you will still need to deal with the downsides of relationships. Let's dive right in.

CHAPTER 4
HOW TO HANDLE CONFLICTS, PEER PRESSURE, AND BULLIES

You may find conflict to be uncomfortable, stressful, or even scary. But learning how to handle conflict in a healthy manner is an important skill that will benefit you in many ways.

Firstly, conflict is a natural part of life. Whether it's with friends, family, or even strangers, you will encounter conflicts throughout your life. Knowing how to handle these conflicts in a mature and effective way will help you maintain healthy relationships and avoid unnecessary drama.

Secondly, handling conflict can help you develop important communication skills. When you encounter a conflict, you must listen to the other person's point of view, express your own thoughts and feelings clearly, and work together to find a solution. These skills will be valuable in your personal and professional life, allowing you to collaborate with others and communicate effectively in a variety of situations.

Thirdly, conflict resolution can help build your confidence and self-esteem. When you are able to handle a conflict in a calm and rational manner, you demonstrate your ability to be assertive and take control of a situation. This can help you feel more confident in your abilities and build a positive self-image.

Lastly, learning how to handle conflict can help you develop empathy and understanding for others. When you are able to see a situation from someone else's point of view, you are more likely to approach conflicts with compassion and a desire to find a mutually beneficial solution. This can help you build stronger, more meaningful relationships with the people in your life.

TIPS FOR HANDLING CONFLICT

Let's talk about a couple of ways you can start practicing conflict resolution and de-escalate arguments before they get out of hand:

- Take a deep breath and try to stay calm when conflict arises. This can help you think more clearly and react less impulsively. Take a moment to calm down and gather your thoughts before responding.
- Listen carefully to the other person's perspective without interrupting. This shows that you respect their point of view and can help you better understand the situation. Be attentive to their words and body language.
- Avoid getting defensive or escalating the conflict. It's easy to become defensive when we feel attacked, but this can make the conflict worse. Instead, try to stay calm and focused on resolving the issue.
- Use "I" statements to express how you feel instead of blaming the other person. For example, saying "I feel hurt when you ignore me" is more effective than saying "You always ignore me." This approach takes ownership of your feelings and avoids blaming the other person.
- Try to understand the other person's feelings and point of view. This can help you see the situation from their perspective and find common ground. Ask questions to clarify their thoughts and feelings.
- Take responsibility for your actions and apologize if necessary. If you've done something wrong, take ownership of it and apologize sincerely. This can go a long way toward resolving the conflict.
- Look for common ground and ways to compromise. Focus on finding a solution that works for both parties, rather than just one side winning.
- Brainstorm solutions together. Collaborate to find solutions that work for both parties. Encourage creativity and open-mindedness.
- Avoid using insults or name-calling. This can escalate the conflict and hurt the other person's feelings.

- Focus on the issue at hand and avoid bringing up past conflicts. Stay focused on the current problem and work toward finding a solution.

WHAT IS PEER PRESSURE?

It's time to talk about something that affects all of us at some point in our lives: peer pressure. So, what is peer pressure? It's when our friends or peers try to influence us to do something that we might not necessarily want to do. It can be something small, like trying a different food, or something more serious, like experimenting with substances you don't want to use.

This can actually take a few different forms and can be either positive or negative. Positive peer pressure is when our friends encourage us to make healthy or positive choices. For example, if your friend encourages you to join a sports team or club, that's positive peer pressure because it's a healthy and productive activity.

Negative peer pressure, on the other hand, can lead us to make harmful or unhealthy choices. Here are some examples of different types of negative peer pressure (Gordon 2020):

Direct Peer Pressure: This is when our friends directly pressure us to do something. For example, if your friend offers you a cigarette and says "Come on, just try it!" that's direct peer pressure.

Indirect Peer Pressure: This is when we feel pressure to do something because of the expectations of our social group. For example, if all your friends are talking about a certain brand of clothing or shoes and you feel like you have to buy them to fit in, that's indirect peer pressure.

Self-Imposed Peer Pressure: This is when we pressure ourselves to fit in or be accepted by our peers. For example, if you feel like you need to be good at a certain sport or activity to be accepted by your friends, that's self-imposed peer pressure.

Cyber Peer Pressure: This is when our friends pressure us to do something through social media or online platforms. For example, if your friends start a group chat and pressure you to join in on cyberbullying someone, that's cyber peer pressure.

Peer pressure can be dangerous because it can lead us to make choices that are not in our best interest. We might feel pressured to do something just to fit in or be accepted by our friends, even if it goes against our own values or beliefs.

STEPS TO DEALING WITH PEER PRESSURE

So, how can we resist peer pressure? First, it's important to be confident in our own beliefs and values. If we know what we stand for, it's easier to say no when our friends try to influence us to do something we're not comfortable with. Here are a few other ways you can handle peer pressure in a healthy way (Gordon, 2020):

- Surround yourself with friends who share your values and beliefs. If your friends respect your choices, you're less likely to feel pressured to do something you're not comfortable with.
- Know your limits. It's okay to set boundaries and say no if you don't want to do something.
- Have an exit strategy. If you're in a situation where you feel uncomfortable or pressured, know how to get out of it safely. Be sure that you come up with a plan to get out of situations you are uncomfortable with before you enter possible peer pressure situations. This could include having a code word you text or call someone with to come pick you up, or an excuse you tell people in order to leave.
- Stay calm and assertive when saying no. Don't let your friends pressure you into doing something you don't want to do.
- Find alternatives. If your friends are pressuring you to do something you don't want to do, suggest an alternative activity that you're more comfortable with.
- Practice saying no. Saying no can be hard, but practicing in a mirror or with a trusted friend can make it easier.
- Focus on your long-term goals. Think about how the choices you make now can impact your future.
- Seek support. Talk to a trusted adult or counselor if you're feeling overwhelmed or unsure of how to handle a situation.
- Be respectful of others' choices. Just because you choose not to do something doesn't mean others can't make their own decisions.
- Remember that you're in control of your own life and choices. Don't let peer pressure dictate your actions.

- Avoid risky situations. If you know a certain activity or situation is risky, it's better to avoid it altogether.
- Stay true to yourself. Don't change who you are or compromise your values just to fit in.
- Be a positive role model for others. Encourage your friends to make healthy and positive choices, and lead by example.

LET'S TALK ABOUT BULLYING

It's important to know what bullying is, how it affects people, and what you can do if you or someone you know is being bullied.

Bullying is *intentional*, repetitive behavior that is meant to harm someone physically, emotionally, or socially.

Bullying can have serious negative effects on teens. It can cause low self-esteem, anxiety, depression, and even physical health problems. Being bullied can make it difficult to focus on schoolwork, have good relationships with others, and feel confident in oneself. There are different types of bullying, and it's important to be aware of them so you can recognize if it's happening to you or someone else (Gordon 2020).

Verbal bullying: This is when someone uses words to hurt someone else. This can include name-calling, teasing, or making fun of someone's appearance or abilities.

Physical bullying: This kind of bullying is when someone uses physical force to hurt or intimidate someone else. This can include hitting, kicking, pushing, or stealing someone's belongings.

Social bullying: This is when someone uses their social power to hurt someone else. This can include spreading rumors, excluding someone from a group, or manipulating others to turn against someone.

Cyberbullying: This type of bullying is when someone uses technology to hurt or harass someone else. This can include sending hurtful messages or images online, spreading rumors on social media, or posting embarrassing photos or videos.

It's important to remember that bullying is never the victim's fault. No one deserves to be bullied and it's not a sign of weakness to ask for help. If you or someone you know is being bullied, here are some things you can do (Orchinik, 2023):

- Report the bullying to a trusted adult. Tell a parent, teacher, counselor, or another adult you trust about what's going on.
- Stay calm and try not to react emotionally. Bullies often thrive on getting a reaction out of their victims.
- Ignore the bully and walk away if possible. Sometimes bullies will lose interest if they don't get a reaction.
- Use confident body language. Stand tall, make eye contact, and speak clearly to show the bully that you are not intimidated.
- Find a friend. Stick with friends or find a trusted adult to be with you in situations where you might encounter a bully.
- Use assertive language. State your boundaries clearly and calmly, and make it known that you will not tolerate the bullying.
- Keep a record of the bullying. Write down what happened, when it happened, and who witnessed it. This can be helpful when reporting the bullying to a teacher or parent.
- Seek support from friends and family. Having people who care about you and can offer emotional support can help you cope with the effects of bullying.
- Practice self-care. Take care of your physical, emotional, and mental health by eating well, getting enough sleep, and doing activities that make you happy.
- Consider joining a support group or seeking counseling. This can help you build confidence, learn coping skills, and develop strategies for dealing with bullying.

THE ROLE OF BYSTANDERS

Bystanders can play an important role in stopping bullying from getting out of hand. Here are a few ways you can help others if you are the one witnessing someone being bullied (Orchinik 2023):

Speak up: If you see someone being bullied, speak up and tell the bully to stop. Use assertive language and make it clear that their behavior is not acceptable.

Get help: If the situation is too dangerous for you to intervene, get help from a teacher, parent, or another adult you trust. They can help to defuse the situation and protect the victim.

Support the victim: Let the victim know that you are there for them and that you support them. Offer to walk with them to class or sit with them at lunch.

Don't join in: It's important to remember that bullying is never okay, even if it seems like everyone else is doing it. Don't join in on the bullying or become part of the problem.

Be a positive influence: Instead of being part of the problem, be part of the solution. Be a positive influence on those around you and stand up for what's right.

Remember, you have the power to make a difference in someone's life by standing up to bullying as a bystander. Don't be afraid to take action and speak out against bullying. Together, we can make our schools and communities a safer and more inclusive place for everyone.

FORGIVENESS, COMPROMISE, AND COMMUNICATION

As a teen, you might find yourself in conflict or disagreement with others from time to time. Some other important skills for handling conflicts include forgiveness, compromise, and effective communication.

It's easy to hold a grudge when someone has wronged you, but *forgiveness* can help you move past the situation and prevent it from escalating. Forgiveness doesn't mean forgetting what happened or excusing the other person's behavior. Instead, it's about choosing to let go of anger and resentment and moving on from the situation.

Another essential skill is *compromise*. In any conflict, it's rare for one side to get everything they want. Compromise means finding a solution that works for everyone involved, even if it means giving up something you want.

Communication is also crucial in diffusing conflicts. When conflicts arise, it's important to communicate openly and honestly with the other person involved. Be clear about your feelings and intentions and listen actively to the other person's perspective.

WAYS TO PRACTICE CONFLICT-RESOLUTION ON A *DAILY* BASIS

Below are a few different exercises and practices you can use to learn conflict-resolution skills!

- Role-playing: Practice conflict-resolution scenarios with a friend or family member. Take turns playing the roles of different people in the conflict and practice using active listening, compromise, and communication to find a resolution.
- Write it out: When you're feeling upset or angry, write out your feelings in a journal. This can help you process your emotions and come up with a plan for how to address the situation.
- Take a break: If you feel like the conflict is getting heated or you need time to cool down, take a break. Go for a walk, listen to music, or do something else you enjoy to take your mind off the situation.

By practicing forgiveness, compromise, effective communication, you can diffuse situations and stop conflicts from escalating even further. These skills take practice, but they can help you build stronger relationships, solve problems more effectively, and create a more positive environment for everyone. Remember, conflicts are a natural part of life, but it's how we handle them that makes all the difference. In the next chapter, we will move on to talk about critical thinking skills and how these skills can help you in your future, decision-making, and more!

CHAPTER 5
CRITICAL THINKING SKILLS

You may not realize it, but critical thinking skills are incredibly important for your future success. Critical thinking means using your brain to carefully analyze and evaluate information, rather than just accepting it at face value. This skill is essential in today's complex and rapidly changing world, where we are bombarded with information from many different sources.

There are many reasons why critical thinking skills are important. First and foremost, critical thinking helps you make better decisions. By carefully evaluating different options and considering their potential outcomes, you can make choices that are more likely to lead to success and happiness. Additionally, critical thinking helps you solve problems more effectively. When faced with a challenge, you can use critical thinking to break the problem down into smaller parts and come up with creative solutions.

In addition to helping you in your personal life, critical thinking skills are also highly valued in the workplace. Employers are looking for workers who can analyze information, solve problems, and make smart decisions. By developing your critical thinking skills, you'll be better prepared for the challenges of the modern workforce and more likely to succeed in your career.

By developing your critical thinking skills through the tips in this chapter, you'll be better equipped to navigate the complex world around you and make informed decisions! Let's get right into it.

UNDERSTANDING LOGICAL FALLACIES

A logical fallacy is an error in reasoning that can make an argument seem more convincing than it really is. There are many different types of logical fallacies, and understanding them is a crucial part of developing your critical thinking skills. Here are a few common types of logical fallacies to watch out for (Nikolopoulou 2023):

Ad Hominem: The Ad Hominem fallacy is when someone tries to attack the person making an argument instead of the argument itself. This is a way of discrediting the speaker rather than engaging with the substance of the argument. For example, if someone says "You can't trust his argument about the environment because he's a vegetarian and doesn't understand how businesses operate," they are attacking the person making the argument rather than addressing the argument itself.

False Dichotomy: The False Dichotomy fallacy is when someone presents only two options to a situation, when in reality, there may be more options available. This can limit the possibilities and ignore other potential outcomes. For example, when someone says "You're either with us or against us," they are limiting the options and ignoring the possibility of a middle ground.

Slippery Slope: The Slippery Slope fallacy is when someone suggests that one small action will lead to a chain of events, eventually resulting in a catastrophic outcome. This is not necessarily true, and it ignores the possibility of alternative outcomes. For example, if someone says, "If we don't stop immigration now, soon the country will be overrun and we'll lose our culture," they are making a slippery slope argument.

Appeal to Authority: The Appeal to Authority fallacy is when someone cites an authority figure to support their argument without providing any evidence. This is not a valid way of arguing because it relies solely on the reputation of the authority figure, without actually providing any substance to the argument. For example, if someone says, "You should buy this product because a celebrity endorsed it," they are making an appeal to authority argument.

Hasty Generalization: The Hasty Generalization fallacy is when someone makes a broad conclusion based on limited or insufficient evidence. This is not a valid way of arguing because it is based on incomplete information and may not reflect the reality of the situation. For example, if someone says, "All athletes are stupid," based on one athlete's mistake, they are making a hasty generalization argument.

EVALUATING SOURCES

Developing your critical thinking skills and learning to evaluate sources for credibility is an essential skill for the modern world. With so much information available at our fingertips, it's more important than ever to be able to distinguish fact from fiction and make informed decisions. By following the tips and strategies in this section, you can become a more discerning critical thinker, better equipped to navigate the complex and ever-changing world around you.

One of the first things you should do when evaluating a source is to consider the author's credentials. Is the author an expert in the field they are writing about? Do they have a history of publishing reliable and accurate information? You can often find this information by doing a quick internet search on the author or organization behind the source.

Another important factor to consider is the bias of the source. Every source has some degree of bias, whether it's political, social, or cultural. To recognize bias, ask yourself what the source's motives might be. What is their agenda? Are they trying to persuade you to believe something or take a certain action? By recognizing bias, you can better understand the source's perspective and adjust your own interpretation accordingly.

When evaluating a source, it's also important to look for corroborating evidence. Does the information presented in the source match up with other reliable sources? Are there any inconsistencies or contradictions in the information presented? By comparing and contrasting different sources, you can get a more accurate and comprehensive understanding of a topic.

Finally, always remember to approach sources with a healthy dose of skepticism. Don't just accept information at face value—ask questions, dig deeper, and don't be afraid to challenge assumptions. By doing so, you can ensure that you are getting accurate, reliable information that you can trust.

PROBLEM-SOLVING AND DECISION-MAKING SKILLS

You're faced with countless decisions and problems to solve every day. Whether it's deciding what to wear to school or solving a complex math problem, problem-solving and decision-making skills are essential for success in life. Here are just a few reasons why these skills are so important (Sigsworth 2022):

Success in school: Being able to solve problems effectively and make informed decisions can help you excel academically.

Career success: Employers value employees who can think critically and make sound decisions.

Personal growth: Developing problem-solving and decision-making skills can help you grow personally by increasing your confidence, independence, and resilience.

Relationships: Being able to communicate effectively and resolve conflicts can lead to stronger, more positive relationships.

Safety: Making good decisions and being able to solve problems can also keep you safe in a variety of situations, from avoiding risky behaviors to knowing how to respond in emergencies.

You will need to learn and develop certain skills in order to learn how to become a better problem-solver and decision-maker.

Let's jump right into some steps you can take to effectively learn to solve a problem (Sigsworth, 2022):

Define the problem: The first step in solving a problem is to clearly define what the problem is. Take some time to think about what the issue is and what specific aspects of it are causing the most trouble.

Gather information: Once you have defined the problem, the next step is to gather as much information as possible about it. This may involve conducting research, talking to others who have dealt with similar issues, or exploring different options and solutions.

Generate possible solutions: Once you have gathered information, it's time to start generating possible solutions. Brainstorm a variety of ideas and approaches, even if they seem unconventional or unlikely to work.

Evaluate the options: After generating a list of possible solutions, evaluate each one carefully. Consider the pros and cons of each option, and think about how each one would impact the situation and those involved.

Choose a solution: Based on your evaluation, choose the best solution to the problem. Make sure that the solution addresses the root cause of the problem and is feasible given the resources and constraints available.

Implement the solution: The final step is to put your chosen solution into action. Develop a plan for how you will implement the solution, including any necessary steps or resources, and start working toward a resolution. Monitor progress and make adjustments as needed until the problem is fully resolved.

Making decisions and solving problems are both important skills to learn. While the process is quite similar, you will need to take a few different steps when making a hard choice. Here are some tips you should keep in mind the next time you are faced with a big decision:

Clarify the decision: Start by being clear about the decision you need to make. Write down the decision you need to make and the different options you are considering.

Set your criteria: Determine what factors are most important to you in making this decision. Consider things like your values, goals, needs, and priorities.

Evaluate the pros and cons: Once you have all the relevant information, evaluate the pros and cons of each option or choice. Consider the advantages and disadvantages, the potential benefits and risks, and any trade-offs you might need to make.

Consider your values and priorities: Your values and priorities play a big role in decision-making. Think about what's important to you and how each option aligns with your values and priorities.

Make a decision and take action: Once you have evaluated all the options and considered your values and priorities, it's time to make a decision. Choose the option that aligns best with your values, priorities, and goals. When you have made your decision, take action. Implement the decision and follow through on any necessary steps.

Reflect and learn: After you make a decision, take some time to reflect on the process and outcome. Think about what you learned and how you can apply those lessons to future decision-making.

HOW TO ASK THE RIGHT QUESTIONS

One key aspect of critical thinking is learning how to ask the right questions. By doing so, you can gather relevant information and make informed decisions. Asking thoughtful questions allows you to get a deeper understanding of a situation or problem. Doing this means you can identify the key issues and come up with effective solutions. For example, if you're trying to decide on a college major, asking questions like "What kind of jobs can I get with this degree?" and "What courses will I need to take?" can help you make an informed decision.

Additionally, asking the right questions helps you evaluate the credibility of sources. With so much information available online, it's important to know how to separate fact from fiction. By asking questions like "Who is the author?" and "What evidence supports this claim?" you can determine if a source is reliable or not.

By seeking out information to support your conclusions, you can avoid making assumptions or jumping to conclusions. Asking the right questions encourages you to think critically and consider different perspectives. This helps you make more informed decisions and avoid potential pitfalls.

Here are a few more tips for learning to ask the right questions and developing this key skill to unlock critical thinking:

Don't settle for surface-level answers: It's easy to accept the first answer that comes to mind or that someone else gives you. However, to truly think critically, you need to challenge assumptions and dig deeper to uncover the underlying reasons and evidence.

Consider multiple perspectives: Before drawing a conclusion or making a decision, try to consider the viewpoints of different people or groups who may be affected. This can help you understand the issue from different angles and develop a more informed opinion.

Keep an open mind: It's important to approach the process of asking questions with an open mind. Don't be too quick to dismiss new information or ideas that don't fit your existing beliefs or assumptions. Instead, be willing to consider new possibilities and adjust your thinking as needed.

Ask follow-up questions: When someone gives you an answer, don't stop there. Instead, ask follow-up questions to gain a deeper understanding of their reasoning and the evidence they are using to support their position. This can also help you identify any gaps in their argument.

PRACTICING OPEN-MINDEDNESS

As a teen boy, it's important to be both skeptical and open-minded. On one hand, you want to approach information and ideas with a healthy dose of skepticism, questioning assumptions and considering alternative viewpoints. On the other hand, you also want to remain open-minded, willing to listen to others and consider new perspectives. Striking a balance between these two approaches can be challenging, but it's essential for critical thinking and personal growth.

Being open-minded also allows you to consider new ideas and perspectives, which can expand your knowledge and challenge your assumptions. When you're open-minded, you're more likely to be empathetic, understand different points of view, and communicate effectively with others. However, being overly open-minded can also lead to gullibility and accepting false information without proper scrutiny.

So, how do you strike a balance between skepticism and open-mindedness? Here are some specific steps you can take:

Examine the evidence: Look at the evidence supporting the information or claim. Is it based on reliable data, scientific research, or other credible sources? Or is it based on personal opinions, anecdotes, or propaganda?

Practice active listening: When engaging with others, practice active listening. This means truly listening to what they have to say and considering their perspective, rather than just waiting for your turn to speak.

Be willing to admit when you're wrong: If new information becomes available that contradicts your beliefs or conclusions, be willing to admit that you may have been wrong. This demonstrates humility and a willingness to learn and grow.

Stay curious: Stay curious and ask questions. Don't be afraid to challenge your own beliefs and assumptions, and seek out new information and perspectives.

PRACTICES FOR APPLYING CRITICAL THINKING SKILLS TO DAILY LIFE

Critical thinking skills aren't just important in academic settings; they're also essential in your daily life. Here are some examples of how critical thinking skills can be applied in everyday situations:

Navigating social media: In today's digital age, social media is a big part of your life. However, not everything you see on social media is true. It's important to use critical thinking skills to evaluate the information you see on social media. For example, you might come across a sensational news story that seems too good (or bad) to be true. Rather than taking it at face value, you should question the source of the story, the evidence presented, and the potential biases involved.

Making financial decisions: Whether you're managing your allowance or starting to earn money through a job, financial decisions are a regular part of your life. Critical thinking can help you evaluate financial choices and avoid costly mistakes. For example, you might be tempted to spend all your money on a new video game, but critical thinking can help you weigh the pros and cons of that decision. Is the game worth the money? Will you regret not saving that money for something else? Thinking through these questions can help you make a better decision.

Evaluating advertisements: Advertisements are designed to convince you to buy a product or service, but they don't always tell the whole truth. Critical thinking can help you evaluate advertisements and make informed choices. For example, you might see an advertisement for a new energy drink that promises to boost your performance in sports. Critical thinking can help you question the evidence presented in the ad, the potential risks involved, and whether the claims made are realistic.

Playing devil's advocate: Practice taking the opposite side of an argument or position. This will help you think critically and consider other perspectives. You don't even need to believe the opposing side of an argument, this is simply a practice to get used to seeing all sides of the situation.

Critical thinking skills will affect every area of your life, including financial decisions, relationships, and even academic success. But let's move on to talk about the importance of respect in all kinds of relationships you will have. In the upcoming chapter you will discover a guide to relationships, kindness, respect, and forgiveness.

CHAPTER 6
RELATIONSHIPS, RESPECT, AND FORGIVENESS

You are at a crucial stage in your life where you are developing your identity and building relationships that will shape your future. These connections include romantic ones, friendships, and family relations. When you are trying to figure yourself out, it can be hard to understand the roles different people will play in your life and develop those connections in a healthy way. This chapter will cover the different people you will have in your life, how to cultivate connections with them, the importance of trust in any relationship, and why it is essential to practice kindness.

Your family relationships are some of the most important you will have in your life. Your parents, siblings, and other family members will be there for you through thick and thin. To build a strong bond with your parents, it is important to learn how to be responsible and respectful toward them. This means following their rules, communicating openly and honestly with them, and always listening to their advice. It's critical to remember that your parents have more life experience than you, so their guidance can be invaluable.

When it comes to your siblings, it is important to be patient and understanding. It can be tricky, but treating your siblings with respect and kindness can go a long way. Try to find common ground with your siblings and be open to compromise. Remember that they will be with you for life, and building a strong connection with them now will pay off in the long run.

Romantic relationships can be exciting, but they can also be challenging. It's important to approach them with care and respect. When starting a relationship, it's important to establish boundaries and communicate openly and honestly with your partner. Remember that the other person is a human being with their own thoughts and feelings. It's essential to be honest and communicative, and always listen to your partner's needs.

In romantic relationships, it's important to respect your partner's boundaries and avoid pressuring them into doing anything they're uncomfortable with. It's also important to recognize that a healthy connection is built on mutual trust, respect, and communication. If you're with someone that makes you feel uncomfortable or unsafe, it's important to seek help and support from trusted adults (Gordon 2021).

Friendships are an essential part of life, and they can have a huge impact on your mental health and well-being. It's important to surround yourself with people who support you and lift you up. Be a good friend by being honest, reliable, and kind. Remember that friendships require effort and communication, so make sure to check in with your friends regularly.

It's also important to recognize that friendships can change over time. As you grow and change, your interests and priorities may shift, and some friendships may naturally fade away. This is a normal part of life, and it's important to be open to new people and experiences.

In all of your connections, it's key to remember that they are a two-way street. Treat others how you want to be treated, and always strive to be a better friend, partner, and family member. By building strong and healthy bonds now, you will set yourself up for a happier, healthier future.

TRUST IS KEY

Relationships are an important part of life, and trust is a key element in building healthy connections with others. In fact, trust is the foundation of all bonds, whether it's with your friends, family, or romantic partner. Without trust, it's hard to establish a deep and meaningful connection with someone.

Mutual trust is essential in any relationship because it creates a foundation of security, openness, and honesty. This means both parties trust each other, that they feel comfortable and secure, and they know that the other person has their best interests at heart. This creates a sense of safety that allows both people to be open and honest with each other.

Trust also promotes effective communication. When both people are able to trust each other, they are more likely to communicate without fear of being judged or rejected. This can help to resolve conflicts and misunderstandings more quickly and effectively, as both parties are willing to listen to each other's perspectives and work together to find a solution.

In addition, mutual trust fosters empathy and understanding. When you both trust each other, you are more likely to show empathy and understanding toward each other's thoughts, feelings, and experiences. This can deepen the relationship and create a sense of closeness and connection.

Let's dive into a few different ways you can practice building mutual trust in your relationships:

Be honest: Honesty is crucial when it comes to building trust. People value honesty, and when you're honest, you show that you're trustworthy. It's important to be truthful with others, even when it's difficult. It's better to be honest because it is simply the right thing to do. When you're honest, it shows that you're willing to be open and transparent and that you value the other person's trust in you.

Be reliable: Reliability is another important aspect of building trust. When you make a commitment, follow through on it consistently. Whether it's showing up on time, completing a task, or keeping a secret, being reliable builds trust. It shows that you're dependable and that you keep your word. When you're reliable, it reassures the other person that they can count on you.

Communicate openly: Communication is key when it comes to building trust. It's important to be open and honest about your thoughts, feelings, and intentions. When you communicate openly, it shows that you're willing to be vulnerable and that you value the other person's thoughts and feelings. Active listening is also an important part of communication. By actively listening, you show that you care about what the other person has to say and that you're willing to hear them out.

Remember, building trust takes time. Trust is not built overnight. It takes time to establish a strong foundation of trust in any relationship. Consistent positive interactions and open communication over an extended period are necessary to build trust. By making a consistent effort to be honest, reliable, open, and respectful, you can build strong, healthy relationships based on trust.

Can you trust everyone?

Trusting others is a necessary aspect of building healthy and fulfilling relationships. However, it can be challenging to know if someone is trustworthy, particularly when you're just getting to know them. Here are some things to consider when assessing whether someone is trustworthy:

Consistency: Trustworthy people are consistent in their words and actions. They don't make promises they can't keep and their behavior is predictable. They don't behave one way with you and then act differently with others. When someone is consistent in their behavior, it creates a sense of stability and reliability, which are essential components of trust.

Honesty: Even when it's challenging, honesty is another key characteristic of trustworthy people. They don't lie or deceive others, and they're transparent in their communication. When someone is honest with you, it creates a sense of safety and security in the relationship.

Dependability: People who are trustworthy follow through on their commitments and show up when they say they will. They are dependable, they don't leave you hanging or cancel plans at the last minute. When someone is dependable, it builds a sense of trust that you can count on them.

Respect: Trustworthy people respect others' boundaries and treat them with kindness and consideration. They don't push you to do something you're uncomfortable with, and they don't ignore your feelings or needs. When someone respects your boundaries, it shows that they value and care about you, which is essential to building trust.

KINDNESS IS COOL

It might seem like the "cool" thing to do is to be rude or dismissive of others. You might see your peers making fun of someone else or putting them down, and you might feel the pressure to join in to fit in with the crowd. But let me tell you something: being kind is cool. In fact, it's one of the most important qualities you can have as a person, and it will benefit you in all areas of your life, including your daily interactions, your academic success, your friendships, and your future.

First of all, let's talk about the importance of kindness in your daily life. When you're kind to others, you're not only making their day better, but you're also improving your own mood and well-being. Studies have shown that performing acts of kindness can actually boost your serotonin levels, which is a hormone that's responsible for feelings of happiness and well-being (Cedars-Sinai, 2019).

Now, let's talk about the importance of kindness in school. When you're kind to your teachers and peers, you create a positive and supportive learning environment. This can lead to better academic performance, as well as stronger relationships with your teachers and classmates. When you're kind to your teachers, they're more likely to go out of their way to help you when you need it. When you're kind to your classmates, you create a sense of community and belonging, which can lead to more positive social experiences.

Kindness is also essential in your friendships. Being kind to your friends shows that you value and care about them, and it can strengthen the bond between you. When you're kind to your friends, they're more likely to be kind to you in return, which creates a positive feedback loop of kindness and support. Additionally, when you're kind to your friends, you create a safe and supportive environment where they feel comfortable opening up to you and sharing their struggles and successes.

Finally, when you're kind to others, you create a positive reputation for yourself. People will remember you as someone who is supportive, caring, and reliable, which can benefit you in all areas of your life, from your future career to your personal relationships.

So, how can you be kind in your daily life, at school, and in your friendships? Here are some tips:

Be empathetic: Try to put yourself in other people's shoes and understand their perspective. This will help you be more understanding and supportive of their feelings and needs.

Be respectful: Treat others with respect, even if you don't agree with them or like them. This means avoiding name-calling, insults, or put-downs.

Be helpful: Offer to help others when they need it, whether it's with home-work, chores, or just a listening ear. Being helpful shows that you care about others and are willing to go out of your way to support them.

Be genuine: Don't try to be someone you're not in order to fit in with others. Instead, be true to yourself and your values, and let your kindness shine through.

WHY IS IT IMPORTANT TO FORGIVE?

Forgiveness is a crucial aspect of maintaining healthy relationships in every aspect of your life. It can be difficult to forgive someone who has hurt you, but holding onto anger and resentment can cause more harm than good.

This does not mean that you have to forget if someone hurt you in the past. It does not mean that their actions were okay or will be accepted again. Forgiveness means letting go of anger and resentment, releasing the two in order to move forward and try to not repeat the same mistakes.

Forgiveness is not just important for maintaining relationships with others; it is also essential for your own well-being. When you hold onto anger and resentment, it can lead to stress, anxiety, and even physical health problems. Forgiveness can help to reduce stress and improve your overall mental and physical health.

Here are some tips and tricks for learning to practice forgiveness:

Recognize your emotions: Forgiveness is an emotional process, and it's crucial to recognize and acknowledge your own feelings. Take time to reflect on what happened, how it made you feel, and why.

Put yourself in the other person's shoes: Empathy is key to forgiveness. Try to understand the other person's perspective and what they may have been going through at the time.

Communicate openly: Talk to the other person about what happened and how it affected you. Be honest and direct, but also listen to their side of the story.

Avoid blame and accusations: Blaming and accusing the other person will only create defensiveness and hinder the forgiveness process. Focus on how you feel and what you need to move forward.

Practice patience: Forgiveness takes time, and it's important to be patient with yourself and the other person. Don't rush the process, and allow yourself time to heal.

Let go of grudges: Holding onto grudges and resentment only hurts you in the long run. Letting go of these negative emotions is a crucial step in the forgiveness process.

Seek support: Forgiveness can be a difficult process to go through alone. Reach out to friends, family, or a therapist for support and guidance.

THE IMPORTANCE OF RESPECT AND BOUNDARIES IN ANY RELATIONSHIP

You're at an age where respect and boundaries are becoming increasingly important. You might have heard these terms thrown around, but what do they actually mean? Let's break it down.

Respect is all about treating others the way you want to be treated. It's about acknowledging and valuing their thoughts, feelings, and boundaries. Boundaries are personal limits that we set for ourselves to protect our physical, emotional, and mental well-being.

Why is respect important in your life and relationships? Because it sets the foundation for healthy interactions with others. Respect fosters trust, communication, and understanding. It shows that you care about the people in your life and their well-being. When you don't show respect, it can lead to conflict, hurt feelings, and damaged relationships.

So, how can you show respect to the people around you? It's not just about respecting authority figures like parents or teachers, but also your friends, siblings, and anyone else in your life. You can start by listening actively and attentively when someone is speaking to you. Try to put yourself in their shoes and understand where they're coming from. Use polite language and manners, like saying "please" and "thank you." And most importantly, respect their boundaries.

But what if you're not receiving the respect you deserve? It's okay to ask for it. You can assert your boundaries by expressing your needs and expectations in a clear and respectful manner. For example, if someone is constantly interrupting you, you can say "Hey, can you please let me finish what I'm saying before you speak?" It's essential to remember that you deserve to be treated with respect and dignity.

Speaking of boundaries, let's talk about their importance. Healthy boundaries help us maintain our physical and emotional safety, as well as our personal independence. They allow us to say no when we're not comfortable with something, and to protect our time and energy. On the other hand, unhealthy boundaries can lead to codependency, low self-esteem, and even abusive situations.

There are actually different types of boundaries, here are a few examples:

Physical boundaries: Personal space, and limits with touch are examples of a physical boundary. It's critical to respect other people's physical boundaries and to assert your own. For example, if someone is standing too close to you or touching you in a way that makes you uncomfortable, you can say "I'm not comfortable with that. Please give me some space."

Emotional boundaries: These boundaries relate to your feelings and emotions. They allow you to separate your own emotions from others and to prioritize your own needs. To set healthy emotional boundaries, you can practice self-care and be honest with yourself and others about how you're feeling. It's also important to respect other people's emotions and not dismiss or minimize them.

Time boundaries: It's crucial to set aside time for yourself and to prioritize your own needs. And time boundaries relate to how to open up your schedule and availability. To set healthy time boundaries, you can schedule self-care activities, prioritize your responsibilities, and communicate your availability to others.

Intellectual boundaries: These boundaries relate to your thoughts and ideas. They allow you to express your own beliefs and opinions without fear of judgment or criticism. To set healthy intellectual boundaries, you can engage in respectful and open-minded discussions, express yourself confidently, and be mindful of others' perspectives.

Now that you know about the different types of boundaries, how do you set healthy boundaries? Here are some tips:

- Be clear and specific about your boundaries. Communicate them in a respectful and assertive manner.
- Be consistent with your boundaries. Don't waiver or compromise them to please others.
- Trust your instincts. If something doesn't feel right, it probably isn't.
- Practice self-care. Taking care of yourself is an important part of setting and maintaining healthy boundaries.

Remember, setting healthy boundaries is a key component of maintaining healthy relationships and protecting your well-being. Don't be afraid to assert your boundaries and prioritize your own needs. By doing so, you're creating a positive and empowering environment for yourself and those around you.

Practice Trust, Forgiveness, and Respect in Daily Life

- Active listening exercises: Practice active listening by having someone speak to you for a few minutes while you listen without interruption. Then, repeat back to them what you heard to ensure you understood their message.
- Gratitude journaling: Write down things you're grateful for each day. This helps build a positive mindset and promotes respect for the good things in your life.
- Apology exercises: Practice apologizing to someone for something you did wrong. Take responsibility for your actions and make amends to show forgiveness and respect.
- Mindfulness exercises: Practice being present in the moment and focusing on your thoughts and emotions. This can help build trust in yourself and others, as well as promote forgiveness and respect for yourself and others.
- Role reversal: Imagine yourself in someone else's shoes and practice showing empathy and understanding for their situation. This can help build respect and trust in your relationships.
- Self-reflection: Take time each day to reflect on your own thoughts and emotions. This can help you better understand yourself and others, and build trust and respect in your relationships.
- Collaborative problem-solving: Work with others to solve problems and make decisions. This can help build trust and respect in your relationships and promote forgiveness and understanding.

The next chapter is all about a topic many teenagers have questions about…
money. How do you make and save money? How do you get your first job?
What are loans? All of these will be answered in the upcoming sections, so
let's dive right in!

CHAPTER 7
ALL ABOUT MONEY

Are you ready to take control of your finances and learn some valuable skills for managing your money? In this chapter, you'll learn about budgeting, getting and keeping a job, and more. These skills are essential for your future success and will help you build a solid foundation for your financial future. Whether you're saving up for a big purchase or planning for your long-term goals, the skills you'll learn in this chapter will be invaluable. So let's dive in and start learning about how to take control of your finances!

TIPS TO GET AND KEEP A JOB

Getting your first job can be an exciting and rewarding experience. Not only can you earn money, but you'll also gain valuable skills and work experience that can help you in the future. However, finding a job as a teenager can be challenging, especially if you have little or no work experience. In this guide, we'll walk you through the steps to finding and getting your first job, including how to find job leads, how to apply, interview tips, workplace etiquette, and other side hustles for teens.

Finding job leads

Before you can apply for a job, you need to find job leads. Here are some ways to find job leads:

Ask around: Ask your friends, family, and neighbors if they know of any job openings.

Check online job boards: Many job openings are listed online, including sites like Indeed, Monster, and LinkedIn.

Visit local businesses: Check out local businesses in your area and ask if they're hiring.

Check with your school: Many schools have job boards or career centers that list job openings for students.

Attend job fairs: Look for job fairs in your area where you can meet with potential employers and learn about job opportunities.

Applying for jobs

Once you've found some job leads, it's time to start applying. Here are some tips for applying for jobs:

Prepare a resume: Even if you have little or no work experience, you can still create a resume that highlights your skills and achievements. Include your contact information, education, any volunteer work or extracurricular activities you've done, and any other relevant experience.

Write a cover letter: A cover letter is a brief letter that introduces you to the employer and explains why you're a good fit for the job. Use the cover letter to highlight your skills and qualifications, and explain why you're interested in the job.

Fill out the application completely: When filling out a job application, make sure to fill out every section completely and accurately. Double-check your spelling and grammar, and make sure your answers are clear and concise.

Follow up: After you've submitted your application, follow up with the employer to make sure they received it. You can do this by calling or emailing the employer to ask about the status of your application.

Interview tips

If you're called in for an interview, congratulations! This means the employer is interested in you and wants to learn more about you. Here are some tips for acing the interview:

Dress appropriately: Dress in business-casual attire for the interview. This shows the employer that you're taking the job seriously.

Thoroughly research the company: Do some research on the company before the interview so you can ask intelligent questions and show the employer that you're interested in the job.

Be on time: Make sure to arrive on time for the interview. Plan to arrive 10-15 minutes early so you have time to check in and prepare yourself.

Practice common interview questions: Prepare for the interview by practicing common interview questions with a friend or family member. Some common questions include the following:

"Tell me about yourself."
"What interests you about this job?"
"What are your strengths?"
"What are your weaknesses?"
"How do you handle stress or pressure?"
"Why should we hire you?"
"Can you give an example of a time when you had to solve a problem?"
"How do you prioritize tasks and manage your time?"

Be confident: During the interview, be confident and enthusiastic. Show the employer that you're excited about the job and eager to learn.

Workplace etiquette

Once you've landed the job, it's important to follow workplace etiquette to ensure that you're successful in your new role. Here are some tips for workplace etiquette:

Be on time: Make sure to arrive on time for your shifts. Being punctual shows the employer that you're reliable and responsible.

Dress appropriately: Follow the dress code and dress appropriately for the job. This shows the employer that you take the job seriously and are committed to being professional.

Respect your coworkers: Treat your coworkers with respect and kindness. Be friendly and supportive, and avoid gossip or negative talk.

Be willing to learn: Be open to learning new skills and taking on new tasks. Ask questions and seek feedback from your coworkers and supervisor.

Communicate effectively: Communicate clearly and respectfully with your coworkers and supervisor. If you have a problem or concern, bring it up in a professional manner.

Other side hustles for teens

If you're looking for additional ways to earn money, there are many side hustles you can explore as a teenager. Here are a few ideas:

Freelance work: If you have skills in writing, graphic design, or other areas, you can offer your services as a freelancer on sites like Fiverr or Upwork.

Pet-sitting or dog-walking: If you love animals, you can offer your services as a pet-sitter or dog-walker in your neighborhood.

Lawn care: Offer your services for lawn care, gardening, or landscaping in your community.

Babysitting: Many parents are looking for responsible teenagers to babysit their children. You can advertise your services on local parenting groups or through word of mouth.

Sell goods online: If you're creative, you can make and sell goods online through platforms like Etsy or Amazon Handmade.

Car washing: Offering your services to family and neighbors as a car washer car be another awesome way to make some extra cash!

THE VALUE OF HARD WORK

In addition to developing a healthy money mindset, it's also essential to understand the value of hard work. Hard work means putting in the effort and dedication to achieve your goals, and it is a critical ingredient for success in any area of life.

When you work hard, you develop a sense of discipline, perseverance, and determination. These qualities help you overcome obstacles and challenges, which are inevitable in any pursuit. Hard work also enables you to build a strong work ethic, which is essential in the workplace. Employers value employees who are willing to put in the effort and go above and beyond to achieve their goals.

Another benefit of hard work is that it helps you develop skills and knowledge in a particular area. When you put in the time and effort to learn and practice a skill, you become better at it. This, in turn, increases your value in the job market and opens up new opportunities for growth and advancement.

In addition to these benefits, hard work also gives you a sense of accomplishment and self-esteem. When you achieve something through hard work, you feel a sense of pride and satisfaction that boosts your confidence and motivation.

To cultivate a strong work ethic, start by setting goals and working toward them consistently. Whether it's improving your grades in school, getting a part-time job, or pursuing a hobby, find something that you are passionate about and put in the time and effort to achieve your goals. Remember to stay focused and disciplined, even when things get challenging.

It's also important to seek out mentors and role models who can guide and inspire you. Talk to people who have achieved success in your field of interest and ask them for advice and feedback. This can help you learn from their experiences and avoid making the same mistakes they did.

LEARNING HOW TO BUDGET AND SAVE MONEY

As you start earning money, it's important to learn how to manage it effectively. Managing your finances may not be a top priority, but it's never too early to learn the importance of budgeting and saving money. Not only will these skills help you achieve financial security in the future, but they will also give you greater control over your life and the ability to make choices that align with your goals and values. In this guide, we will discuss why budgeting and saving money are important, different methods for budgeting, and tips for saving money.

Here are a few reasons why learning to budget and effectively manage your money is so important (Better Money Habits 2023):

Financial security: Budgeting and saving money can help you achieve financial security. Having money saved for emergencies or unexpected expenses can provide peace of mind and reduce stress.

Independence: As a teenager, you may rely on your parents or guardians for financial support. However, by learning how to budget and save money, you can gain greater independence and the ability to make your own financial decisions.

Achieving goals: Whether it's buying a car, paying for college, or traveling, having a budget and saving money can help you achieve your goals and make your dreams a reality.

Developing good habits: Learning how to budget and save money at a young age can help you develop good financial habits that will benefit you throughout your life.

Different methods for budgeting

There are actually a lot of different ways you can manage and budget your money. It doesn't really matter which method you choose, as long as it works for you and your lifestyle (Luthi 2020):

The 50/30/20 Rule: This budgeting method involves allocating 50% of your income toward necessities (such as rent, food, and bills), 30% toward discretionary spending (such as entertainment and hobbies), and 20% toward savings or debt repayment.

Envelope Method: With this method, you allocate cash into envelopes for different expenses, such as groceries, entertainment, and transportation. Once the money in an envelope is gone, you cannot spend any more money in that category.

Zero-Based Budgeting: This method involves assigning a specific dollar amount for each expense category and making sure that your income minus expenses equals zero at the end of each month.

Automated Budgeting: This involves using an app or software to track your expenses and automate savings. You can set up automatic transfers to your savings account or investment account, making it easier to save money.

Tips for saving money

Set financial goals: Set specific financial goals for yourself, such as saving for a car or college. This will give you a clear target to work toward and help you stay motivated.

Reduce unnecessary expenses: Take a look at your expenses and identify areas where you can cut back. For example, you can bring your lunch to school instead of buying food, or reduce your spending on entertainment.

Shop smart: When shopping for groceries or other items, look for sales and discounts. You can also use coupons or buy items in bulk to save money.

Avoid impulse buying: Before making a purchase, ask yourself if you really need the item and if it aligns with your financial goals. Avoid impulse buying and take the time to consider your options.

Start small: Saving money can be challenging, especially if you're just starting out. Start by setting aside a small amount of money each week or month, and gradually increase the amount over time.

Budgeting and saving money may seem daunting at first, but with practice and dedication, these skills can help you achieve financial security, independence, and your goals. By choosing a budgeting method that works for you and following these tips for saving money, you'll be on your way to financial success in no time. Remember, it's never too early to start building good financial habits that will benefit you for the rest of your life.

UNDERSTANDING LOANS

Loans are a way of borrowing money to purchase something that you don't have the money for yet. Loans could be for purchasing a car, paying for college, or even starting a business. It's important to understand the different types of loans available, how they work, and their potential risks and benefits. In this guide, we will explore the different types of loans, why some are good, an introduction to credit cards, and more.

Let's dive into some of the different types of loans available (Pentis & Evans 2021):

Personal Loans: These kinds of loans are unsecured loans that you can use for any purpose, such as consolidating debt, paying for a wedding, or covering emergency expenses. These loans don't require collateral, meaning you don't have to put up any assets, such as a car or house, to secure the loan. However, since they are unsecured, they usually come with higher interest rates than secured loans.

Student Loans: These are used to pay for college or other educational expenses. They can be obtained through the government or private lenders. Government loans tend to have lower interest rates and more flexible repayment options than private loans. Private loans can have variable interest rates and require a credit check or a co-signer.

Auto Loans: Otherwise known as car loans, these are used to finance the purchase of a vehicle. They can be obtained through the dealership, bank, or credit union. The loan is secured by the car, meaning if you default on payments, the lender can repossess the vehicle. The interest rate for an auto loan can vary depending on your credit score and the term of the loan.

The thing is, not all loans are bad, in fact some can really work in your favor. Here are a couple ways you can use loans to your advantage:

Building credit: Taking out a loan and making payments on time can help build your credit score. A good credit score is important for obtaining loans, credit cards, and other financial products in the future. Building good credit takes time, so starting early can be beneficial in the long run.

Funding opportunities: Loans can provide opportunities for funding that wouldn't otherwise be available. For example, a student loan can allow you to attend college and pursue a career that may have been out of reach otherwise.

Emergency situations: Loans can be useful in emergency situations, such as unexpected medical bills or car repairs. Having access to a loan can provide peace of mind and prevent financial stress during these situations.

INTRODUCTION TO CREDIT CARDS

Credit cards are a type of loan that allows you to borrow money for purchases. The money you borrow must be paid back, usually with interest. Credit cards can be a useful tool for building credit and making purchases, but they can also be risky if not used responsibly.

Credit cards work by allowing you to borrow money up to a certain limit. You can use the card to make purchases, and the amount you spend is added to your balance. Each month, you receive a statement that shows your balance, minimum payment, and due date. If you pay the full balance by the due date, you won't incur any interest charges. However, if you carry a balance, you'll be charged interest on the amount you owe. There are some risks you will need to look out for, including:

High-interest rates: Credit cards can have high-interest rates, especially if you have a low credit score. If you don't pay off your balance in full each month, the interest charges can quickly accumulate, making it harder to pay off the debt.

Overspending: Credit cards can be tempting to use for purchases that you can't afford. This can lead to overspending and accumulating debt that can be difficult to pay off.

Late payment fees: If you don't make your credit card payment on time, you can be charged late payment fees, which can add up quickly and make it harder to pay off your balance.

WHAT IS FINANCIAL INDEPENDENCE?

Financial independence is the ability to support yourself without relying on anyone else financially. Achieving financial independence means that you have the freedom to live the life you want, without being limited by financial constraints. In this guide, we'll explore what financial independence is and why it's an important goal to work toward as a teen even before entering your adult years.

There are many reasons why financial independence is crucial for teenage boys. Here are a few:

Freedom and flexibility: When you're financially independent, you have the freedom to make your own decisions about your life. You can choose where you want to live, what kind of job you want to have, and how you want to spend your time. You won't be limited by financial constraints or dependent on someone else's income.

Personal growth: Achieving financial independence requires discipline, hard work, and a willingness to learn. By working toward this goal, you will develop important life skills and qualities like perseverance, responsibility, and self-reliance. These qualities will help you grow and mature as a person, and prepare you for the challenges of adult life.

Opportunities: Financial independence opens up new opportunities and possibilities. You'll be able to take risks and pursue your dreams without worrying about money. You can start your own business, travel the world, or pursue a career in a field that you're passionate about.

Peace of mind: When you're financially independent, you won't have to worry about financial stress or instability. You'll have the peace of mind that comes with knowing that you can support yourself and your future family.

TIPS FOR ACHIEVING FINANCIAL INDEPENDENCE

Now that you understand why financial independence is important, let's explore how to work toward this goal.

Create a budget: This is one of the very first steps toward financial independence. Start by taking a look at the budgeting section above and figuring out a method that works for you!

Save early and often: The earlier you start saving, the better. Even if you're only able to save a small amount each month, it will add up over time. Aim to save at least 10% of your income each month.

Invest wisely: Investing can be a great way to grow your wealth *over time*. However, it's important to invest wisely and understand the risks involved. Consider investing in a diverse range of assets, such as stocks, bonds, and real estate.

Choose a career path wisely: Choosing a career path that aligns with your interests and passions can lead to a fulfilling and financially rewarding life. Research different career options and consider the earning potential and job outlook before making a decision.

Avoid debt: Debt can be a major obstacle to financial independence. Avoid taking on debt for non-essential expenses, like luxury items or vacations. If you do need to take on debt, make sure you have a plan to pay it off quickly.

Be patient: Achieving financial independence takes time and patience. It's important to stay focused on your goals and not get discouraged by setbacks or obstacles along the way. Keep working hard, save as much as you can, and make smart financial decisions.

DAILY PRACTICES TO LEARN HOW TO MANAGE YOUR MONEY

- Use cash more often: Using cash instead of credit or debit cards can help you stay within your budget. You can withdraw a fixed amount of cash every week and use it for your daily expenses.
- Look for ways to increase your income: Find ways to increase your income, such as taking on a part-time job or starting a small business. This will help you achieve your financial goals faster.
- Prioritize your spending: Make a list of your priorities and allocate your money accordingly. This will help you focus on the things that matter most to you and avoid overspending on things that aren't as important.
- Review your expenses regularly: Take some time every week or month to review your expenses and see if there are any areas where you can cut back. This will help you stay on track with your budget and make adjustments as needed.
- Create a budget challenge: Challenge yourself to stick to a budget for a certain amount of time, such as a week or a month. This can help you become more aware of your spending habits and identify areas where you can cut back.
- Practice delayed gratification: Learn to delay gratification by saving up for big purchases instead of buying them on credit. This will help you avoid debt and teach you the value of saving and patience.

Money isn't the only thing you will need to learn to manage as you prepare to enter adulthood. Time is just as important. In the next chapter you will discover a guide to time management and setting effective goals to reach future success.

CHAPTER 8
TIPS TO MANAGE YOUR TIME AND SET GOALS

As a teenager, you have many responsibilities, such as school, extracurricular activities, family obligations, and social life. It can be challenging to balance all of these responsibilities and still have time for yourself. It can be even harder to work for your future and figure out what you want to do with your life. This is where time management and goal setting come in.

Time management is the process of planning and organizing how you allocate your time effectively to accomplish your goals. With good time management, you can prioritize your tasks, avoid procrastination, and make the most of your time. It can help you reduce stress, increase productivity, and achieve your desired outcomes.

Setting goals is also crucial for success. Goals provide direction, motivation, and focus. They give you something to strive for and a sense of accomplishment when you achieve them. Setting goals can help you clarify your priorities, identify your strengths and weaknesses, and improve your decision-making skills.

As a teenage boy, you are at a critical stage in your life where the choices you make can impact your future. Learning how to manage your time effectively and set goals can set you up for success in all aspects of your life, including academic, personal, and professional. It can help you develop self-discipline, build confidence, and increase your chances of achieving your dreams. So let's jump right in!

HOW TO SET *EFFECTIVE* AND *REALISTIC* GOALS

It's not enough to simply think of and set goals. You need to set effective and realistic goals that you can accomplish. In this section, we'll explore some practical tips on how to set effective and realistic goals.

Assess your current situation: First up, assess your current situation. What resources and abilities do you have? What challenges or obstacles might you face in achieving your goals? Understanding your current situation will help you set goals that are realistic and achievable.

Be specific: The next step to setting effective goals is to be specific about what you want to achieve. Instead of setting vague goals like "get better at math," be specific about what you want to accomplish, such as "improve my math grade from a C to a B."

Make your goals measurable: Your goals should be measurable so that you can track your progress and know when you've achieved them. For example, instead of setting a goal to "get in shape," set a goal to "run a mile in under 8 minutes in the next month."

Break down big goals into smaller ones: Breaking down big goals into smaller ones can make them more manageable and less overwhelming. For example, if your goal is to write a novel, break it down into smaller goals like "write 500 words per day" or "finish one chapter per week."

Consider your resources: When setting realistic goals, it's important to consider your resources. This includes your time, money, and any other resources necessary to achieve your goals. For example, if your goal is to travel to a foreign country, consider how much money and time you need to save, and plan accordingly.

Use SMART criteria: The SMART criteria can help you set realistic goals. SMART stands for Specific, Measurable, Achievable, Relevant, and Time-bound. Make sure your goals meet each of these criteria.

Consider your motivation: When setting goals, consider what motivates you. What drives you to achieve your goals? Understanding your motivation can help you set goals that are meaningful and relevant to you.

Visualize your goals: Visualizing your goals can help you stay focused and motivated. Imagine yourself achieving your goals and how it will feel. Visualize yourself taking the necessary steps to achieve your goals.

Plan for obstacles: When setting realistic goals, it's important to plan for obstacles. Think about what challenges or obstacles you might face in achieving your goals, and come up with a plan to overcome them. This will help you stay focused and motivated, even when faced with setbacks.

Get feedback: Getting feedback from others can be helpful in setting realistic goals. Talk to people who have achieved similar goals and ask for their advice. They may have insights that can help you set more realistic goals.

Write down your goals: Writing down your goals can help you remember them and stay committed to achieving them. Put your goals somewhere visible, like a sticky note on your computer or a poster on your wall.

Review your goals regularly: Reviewing your goals regularly can help you stay on track and make any necessary adjustments. Set aside time each week or month to review your goals and assess your progress.

ESSENTIAL TIME MANAGEMENT STRATEGIES

Do you ever feel like there just aren't enough hours in the day? With school, extracurriculars, and social activities, it can be tough to fit everything in. That's where time management comes in. There are many different time management techniques that you can use to help you make the most of your time and achieve your goals. Here are some of the most popular techniques and how to use them effectively (Morin 2019):

The Pomodoro Technique: This time management strategy involves working for 25 minutes, then taking a 5-minute break. After four cycles, take a longer break. To use this technique effectively, set a timer for 25 minutes and work on a single task until the timer goes off. Then, take a 5-minute break to stretch, grab a snack, or do something else to recharge your brain. Repeat this cycle four times, then take a longer break of 15-30 minutes. This technique helps you stay focused and avoid burnout.

Eat the Frog: This technique involves tackling your most difficult or important task first thing in the morning. To use this technique effectively, make a list of your tasks for the day and prioritize them based on importance and urgency. Then, choose the most difficult or important task and focus on completing it before moving on to other tasks. This technique helps you overcome procrastination and build momentum for the rest of your day.

Time Blocking: This method involves scheduling blocks of time for specific tasks. To use this technique effectively, block out time in your calendar for each task on your to-do list. Be realistic about how much time each task will take, and make sure to include breaks and time for unexpected interruptions. This technique helps you stay focused and avoid multitasking.

The Eisenhower Matrix: This time management technique involves categorizing your tasks based on importance and urgency. To use this technique effectively, make a list of your tasks and categorize them as follows: urgent and important, important but not urgent, urgent but not important, and not urgent and not important. Then, focus on completing the tasks in the urgent and important category first, followed by the important but not urgent category. This technique helps you prioritize your tasks and make sure you're focusing on the most important ones first.

The 2-Minute Rule: This strategy involves tackling small tasks that can be completed in 2 minutes or less right away. To use this technique effectively, whenever you come across a task that can be completed quickly, do it immediately rather than putting it off. This technique helps you avoid procrastination and build momentum for the rest of your day.

Delegating tasks can be another great way to manage your time more effectively and get more done. It can also help you develop leadership skills and build stronger relationships with your friends and family. Identify tasks that can be delegated. Look for tasks that don't require your specific expertise or skills, or tasks that you don't enjoy doing. These might include household chores, school projects, or community service activities. Here are some steps to start delegating tasks to manage time better:

- Choose the right person for the task: Consider the skills and abilities of the people around you and choose someone who is capable of doing the task well. If you're not sure who to ask, consider asking for recommendations from others or asking for volunteers.
- Be clear about expectations: Make sure the person you delegate the task to understands what is expected of them, including the deadline, the level of quality expected, and any specific instructions.

If necessary, provide additional guidance or training to ensure that they can complete the task successfully.

- Provide support and feedback: Check in regularly with the person you delegated the task to and offer support and feedback as needed. This can help them stay on track and feel more confident in completing the task.

EXERCISES TO PRACTICE GOAL SETTING AND TIME MANAGEMENT

Let's jump right into some ways you can practice time management, prioritization, and goal setting! Below are some exercises and games you can start using to get into the habit of using these skills:

- Time logging: This exercise helps you understand how you spend your time and identify areas where you can improve your time management skills. Keep a log of how you spend your time for a week or two, and then analyze the data to see where you are spending too much time on unimportant tasks or where you can be more efficient. This exercise can help you develop a better understanding of how you use your time and identify ways to make better use of it.
- Daily goal setting: This exercise helps you prioritize your goals and tasks each day to make the most of your time. At the beginning of each day, create a list of tasks and goals that you need to accomplish that day, and then prioritize them in order of importance. Throughout the day, check off each task as you complete it. This exercise can help you stay focused and productive throughout the day.
- Prioritization puzzle: This exercise helps you understand the importance of prioritizing tasks and goals in order to be more efficient and effective in managing your time. First, create a list of tasks and goals that you need to complete, then cut the item into its own piece. Mix up the pieces and then try to put them in order of priority as quickly as possible. This exercise can help you practice critical thinking skills, and it can also help you identify which tasks are most important to focus on first.

- Time tracker: This game helps you learn how to manage your time effectively by setting realistic time limits for specific tasks and goals. Choose a goal that you want to accomplish, and then set a timer for the amount of time you think it will take to complete the task. Then, try to complete the goal within the time limit. If you finish early, you can reward yourself with a short break or some other type of incentive. This exercise can help you develop a sense of urgency and focus, which are important skills for managing your time effectively.
- Goal-setting bingo: This game helps you identify and prioritize your goals, and it also helps you stay motivated to achieve them. Create a bingo board with different goals written in each square. These can be short-term or long-term goals, such as "get an A on a test" or "learn a new skill." Then, as you accomplish each goal, mark off the corresponding square on the bingo board. Once you get a row or a column marked off, reward yourself with something you enjoy. This exercise can help you stay motivated and focused on your goals, and it can also help you prioritize which goals are most important to you.

Learning to set goals and manage your time in an effective way will help propel you into your future with the tools you need for success. Another essential skill all teens need to learn is how to take care of your body. In the next chapter, we will talk all things physical and mental health.

CHAPTER 9
PERSONAL HEALTH AND HYGIENE

It can sometimes feel like there are a million things you need to keep track of each day. Between school, sports, social activities, and family responsibilities, it can be easy to let your personal hygiene and health fall by the wayside. However, taking care of your mental and physical health is crucial for feeling your best and achieving your goals. In this chapter, we'll explore the importance of personal hygiene and health, and provide tips and strategies for taking care of yourself both inside and out. From building healthy habits to finding support when you need it, this chapter will help you develop the skills and knowledge you need to live your best life. So let's dive in and learn how to take care of your mind and body, and feel your best every day.

PERSONAL HYGIENE

Taking care of your personal hygiene is an important part of staying healthy and feeling confident. It involves a variety of practices, from grooming to bathing, skin and hair care, and more. By developing good hygiene habits, you can keep your skin and hair looking and feeling great, and avoid unpleasant odors and infections. Here are some tips and strategies for maintaining good personal hygiene in each of these areas (Old Mt Pleasant Dentistry 2020):

Grooming: Regular grooming can help you look and feel your best. This includes things like brushing your teeth twice a day, flossing daily, and keeping your nails trimmed and clean. When it comes to your hair, consider a style that is easy to manage and maintain. A clean, well-groomed appearance can help you feel more confident in yourself and make a great first impression.

Bathing: Taking a shower or bath regularly can help you feel clean and refreshed. Aim to bathe at least once a day, or more often if you're particularly active or sweaty. Use soap and warm water to clean your body thoroughly, paying special attention to areas like your armpits, groin, and feet. Remember to clean behind your ears and under your fingernails, as bacteria can easily collect in these areas.

Skin care: Taking care of your skin can help prevent acne and other skin problems. Wash your face twice a day with a gentle cleanser, and moisturize regularly to keep your skin soft and hydrated. If you spend a lot of time outdoors, be sure to use sunscreen to protect your skin from the sun's harmful UV rays. If you have acne, consider using a product specifically designed to treat it, and avoid picking at your skin to prevent scarring.

Hair care: Keeping your hair clean and well-groomed can help you look and feel your best. Shampoo your hair regularly, and use a conditioner to keep it soft and manageable. If you have long hair, be sure to brush it regularly to prevent tangles and knots. Consider using styling products to keep your hair looking neat and well-maintained.

Clothing: Wearing clean clothes can help you feel fresh and confident. Be sure to wash your clothes regularly, and change your underwear and socks every day. If you participate in sports or other activities that cause you to sweat, consider changing your clothes more often to prevent odors. Also, choose clothing that fits well and makes you feel comfortable and confident.

Oral hygiene: Taking care of your teeth and gums is crucial for maintaining good overall health. Brush your teeth twice a day for at least two minutes each time, using a fluoride toothpaste. Floss between your teeth daily to remove plaque and food particles that can cause cavities and gum disease. Consider using a mouthwash to freshen your breath and kill bacteria that can cause bad breath.

Deodorant: Use a deodorant or antiperspirant to help prevent body odor. Apply it after showering or bathing, and reapply as needed throughout the day.

Shaving: If you shave, be sure to use a clean razor and shaving cream or gel. Shave in the direction of hair growth to prevent razor burn and ingrown hairs. If you have a beard or mustache, keep it trimmed and well-groomed.

A GUIDE TO NUTRITION

Eating a healthy, balanced diet is crucial for providing your body with the energy and nutrients it needs to grow, develop, and function properly. As a teenage boy, you need plenty of calories to fuel your growing body, as well as a variety of vitamins, minerals, and other nutrients to support your physical and mental health. Here are some tips and strategies for eating a healthy, balanced diet and maintaining good nutrition (John Muir Health 2023):

Eat a variety of foods: To get all the nutrients your body needs, aim to eat a variety of foods from each of the five food groups: fruits, vegetables, grains, protein foods, and dairy. Each group provides different nutrients that your body needs, so try to include a variety of colors, textures, and flavors in your meals and snacks.

Choose whole foods: Whole foods are minimally processed and contain more nutrients than highly processed foods. Choose whole grains like brown rice and whole wheat bread, and choose fresh or frozen fruits and vegetables over canned or processed ones. Processed and sugary foods can contribute to weight gain and poor health, so it's important to limit your intake of these foods.

Get plenty of protein: Protein is important for building and repairing muscle tissue, and can help you feel full and satisfied. Choose lean protein sources like chicken, fish, beans, nuts, and tofu, and aim for at least 2-3 servings per day.

Include healthy fats: Healthy fats, like those found in nuts, seeds, avocados, and fatty fish, can help support brain health and keep you feeling full and satisfied. Aim for 2-3 servings of healthy fats per day.

Limit sugary drinks: Drinking plenty of water is crucial for staying hydrated and supporting your body's functions. Aim for at least 8-10 cups of water per day, and limit sugary drinks like soda and juice.

Plan ahead: Planning your meals and snacks ahead of time can help ensure that you have healthy options on hand when you need them. Try meal prepping on the weekends, or packing healthy snacks like nuts, fruit, or yogurt to take with you on the go.

Don't restrict yourself: While it's important to make healthy choices, it's also important to enjoy the foods you love. Don't restrict yourself too much or follow a strict diet, as this can lead to unhealthy eating patterns and feelings of guilt or shame around food. Allow yourself to indulge in moderation and focus on balance and moderation.

Get plenty of fiber: Fiber is important for keeping your digestive system healthy, and can help you feel full and satisfied after meals. Choose high-fiber foods like fruits, vegetables, whole grains, and beans, and aim for at least 25-30 grams of fiber per day.

THE IMPORTANCE OF EXERCISE AND SLEEP

Exercise and sleep are essential for your overall health and well-being. Exercise can help you stay fit, improve your mood, and reduce stress, while sleep can help you feel refreshed and energized. Here are some tips to help you get more exercise and better sleep (John Muir Health 2023):

Get moving: There are many ways to get more movement in your day. You can join a sports team, take a dance or martial arts class, go for a walk or bike ride, or simply play outside with friends. The important thing is to find something you enjoy and that gets you moving.

Strength training: Strength training is also important for overall fitness. You can do bodyweight exercises like push-ups, squats, and lunges, or use resistance bands or weights. Be sure to start with lighter weights and proper form to avoid injury.

Cardiovascular exercise: Cardiovascular exercise, like running, biking, or swimming, can help improve your endurance and overall fitness. Aim for at least 30 minutes of moderate-intensity cardiovascular exercise per day, or more if you can.

Stretching: Stretching can help improve your flexibility and reduce your risk of injury. Be sure to stretch before and after exercise, and aim to stretch all major muscle groups.

Getting enough sleep is crucial for your health and well-being. Aim for 8-10 hours of sleep per night, and try to keep a consistent sleep schedule, even on weekends. Here are a few ways you can improve your sleep and raise your energy levels:

Establish a nighttime routine: Establishing a bedtime routine can help you wind down and prepare for sleep. Try to avoid screens for at least an hour before bed, and engage in relaxing activities like reading or taking a warm bath.

Create a sleep-conducive environment: Creating a sleep-conducive environment can also help you get better sleep. Keep your bedroom cool, quiet, and dark, and invest in a comfortable mattress and pillow.

Avoid caffeine and sugary foods before bed: Consuming caffeine or sugary foods and drinks before bed can interfere with your ability to fall asleep and stay asleep. It's best to avoid these foods and drinks, especially in the hours leading up to when you want to head to bed.

Get plenty of sunlight during the day: Exposure to natural sunlight during the day can help regulate your body's internal clock and improve your sleep quality. Try to spend some time outside each day, or consider using a light box during the winter months when sunlight is limited.

WHAT IS BODY IMAGE?

Body image refers to the way you feel about your physical appearance. It's common for teens, both boys and girls, to struggle with body image issues. Many factors can contribute to negative body image, including social media, peer pressure, and unrealistic beauty standards portrayed in the media.

It's important to remember that having a negative body image doesn't make you any less of a man. It's okay to feel insecure about your appearance, but it's important to learn to love and accept yourself just the way you are.

Here are some tips to help improve your body image:

Focus on your strengths: Instead of dwelling on your flaws, focus on your strengths and things you like about your appearance. Celebrate the things that make you unique and special.

Practice gratitude: Take time each day to reflect on things you're grateful for. Focusing on the positive things in your life can help shift your mindset away from negative self-talk.

Take a break from social media: Social media can be a breeding ground for unrealistic beauty standards and negative thoughts about your body image. Consider taking a break from social media or unfollowing accounts that make you feel bad about yourself.

Practice mindfulness: Mindfulness involves paying attention to the present moment without judgment. Practicing mindfulness can help you focus on the positive aspects of your life and reduce negative self-talk. You can practice mindfulness by simply taking breaks to recenter yourself and take deep breaths throughout the day.

Seek help if needed: If having negative body image is affecting your daily life or causing distress, don't hesitate to seek professional help. Talk to a trusted adult or health care provider who can help you find resources and support.

Surround yourself with positive body image messages: Seek out positive messages and role models that promote a healthy body image. This can include following body-positive social media accounts, reading books or articles about body positivity, and surrounding yourself with positive role models who celebrate diverse body types.

MENTAL HEALTH—WHAT IS SELF-CARE?

It's important to take care of your mental health just as much as your physical health. Mental health refers to how you feel, think, and behave, and it's just as important as your physical health. In fact, mental health and physical health are connected, and taking care of your mental health can actually improve your physical health too.

Self-care is an important part of taking care of your mental health. It can include things like taking a break when you need it, doing something you enjoy, or spending time with friends and family. Here are some tips for practicing self-care and improving your mental health:

Know the signs of mental health issues: It's important to know the signs of mental health issues, such as anxiety and depression, so you can seek help if you need it.

Signs of anxiety and depression can include excessive worrying, feeling on edge, and experiencing physical symptoms like sweating, shaking, or rapid heart rate. Depression can manifest in different ways, but some common signs include feeling sad or hopeless, losing interest in things you used to enjoy, and having difficulty sleeping or concentrating. You may also experience physical symptoms like fatigue or changes in appetite.

Practice mindfulness: Mindfulness is a powerful technique that can help you achieve a more positive outlook on life. By practicing mindfulness, you can learn to focus on the present moment, instead of getting caught up in worries about the past or future. This can be especially helpful for reducing stress and anxiety, which are common issues for many teens.

One of the easiest ways to practice mindfulness is to focus on your breath. Sit comfortably in a quiet space and take a few deep breaths. Try to focus your attention solely on your breath as you inhale and exhale. You may find that your mind starts to wander, and that's okay. Simply notice the thought, let it go, and bring your attention back to your breath.

Take breaks when you need them: When you're feeling stressed or overwhelmed, it's essential to take a break and give yourself time to recharge. This could mean stepping outside for a short walk or sitting down in a quiet space for some deep breathing exercises. Taking a power nap can also be a great way to rejuvenate yourself and improve your productivity when you return to your tasks. This is one of the best ways to practice self-care in a simple way. It's important to remember that taking a break doesn't mean you're being lazy or unproductive. On the contrary, taking breaks can help you perform better in the long run. Studies show that taking regular breaks can improve focus, creativity, and decision-making skills.

Do things you enjoy: It's essential to take some time out of your busy schedule to do things that bring you joy and happiness. Engaging in activities that you enjoy can help reduce stress and improve your overall well-being. So, don't forget to make time for the things that you love.

There are many activities you can try, such as reading a book, listening to your favorite music, watching a movie, or playing video games. These activities can help you relax and unwind after a long day or week. You may also want to consider exploring new hobbies or interests to find something that you truly enjoy.

Practice self-compassion: Practicing self-compassion is an important aspect of maintaining good mental health. Being kind to yourself and not being too hard on yourself can help you build resilience and cope with challenging situations. Self-compassion can also involve taking care of yourself when you're feeling down or overwhelmed. This could mean taking a break from work or school to do something relaxing, such as taking a warm bath, practicing meditation, or doing some light exercise.

Remember, showing kindness to yourself is not about making excuses for your mistakes or weaknesses. It's about recognizing your humanity and treating yourself with the same kindness and care that you would extend to others.

CHAPTER 10
STAYING SAFE AND RESPONSIBLE ONLINE

As you navigate the world of social media, online gaming, and internet browsing, it's important to be aware of the potential risks to your safety and privacy. Have you heard of the term "digital footprint?" It refers to the trail of information you leave behind online, such as your social media profiles, emails, and search history. It's important to be aware of your digital footprint because it can have a significant impact on your future.

When you apply for jobs or colleges, for example, employers and admissions officers may search for your name online. They could come across embarrassing photos, inappropriate comments, or other content that could hurt your chances of getting hired or accepted. Your digital footprint can also affect your relationships and personal life.

In this chapter, we'll explore the different ways you can protect yourself online and stay in control of your personal information. From creating strong passwords to understanding the dangers of sharing sensitive information, you'll learn practical tips and strategies to help you stay safe and secure in the digital world. So let's dive in and start exploring the world of online safety and privacy!

A GUIDE TO ONLINE PRIVACY

Whether you're browsing social media, playing video games, or doing homework, it's important to be aware of the potential risks to your online privacy. When you're online, you're constantly sharing personal information. This can include your name, age, location, interests, and more. While sharing some information is necessary for certain online activities, it's important to be aware of the risks involved. Your personal information can be used by hackers, scammers, and identity thieves to commit fraud or steal your identity.

There are several steps you can take to protect your personal information and mobile devices, including setting strong passwords, managing your social media privacy settings, and being cautious about what you share online. Here are a few different ways to get started (Pearl 2022):

Setting strong passwords: Setting strong passwords is an important step in protecting your personal information online. A strong password should be at least 12 characters long and include a mix of letters, numbers, and symbols. Avoid using easily guessable information, such as your name or birthdate, as part of your password. Instead, consider using a passphrase or combination of random words that are easy for you to remember but difficult for others to guess. It's also important to use different passwords for different accounts. If one of your accounts is compromised, using different passwords ensures that your other accounts are still secure.

For your phone, using another unique passcode or biometric authentication, such as a fingerprint or facial recognition, is an important step in securing your mobile device. This ensures that if your device is lost or stolen, no one can access your personal information.

Use two-factor authentication: Two-factor authentication provides an extra layer of security by requiring you to enter a code sent to your phone or email in addition to your password.

Avoiding public Wi-Fi networks: Public Wi-Fi networks are often unsecured, which means that anyone can potentially access your device and personal information. Avoid using public Wi-Fi networks to access sensitive information such as your bank account or personal email.

Updating your software regularly: Regularly updating your software is important for keeping your device secure. Software updates often include security patches and bug fixes that can help protect your device from vulnerabilities.

Being cautious about app permissions: When you download an app, it often requests certain permissions to access your device's features such as your camera or microphone. Be cautious about granting these permissions and only download apps from reputable sources.

Use a virtual private network (VPN): A VPN encrypts your internet connection, making it more difficult for others to intercept your data. Consider using a VPN when using public Wi-Fi networks or when accessing sensitive information.

STAYING SAFE FROM ONLINE PREDATORS

Online predators are individuals who use the internet to target and exploit children and teenagers for their own personal gain. These predators may use social media, chat rooms, or other online platforms to gain access to young people and establish a relationship with them. It is important to be aware of the dangers of online predators and take steps to protect yourself from them.

Here are a few ways you can work to protect yourself from online predators (Pearl 2022):

Avoid interactions with strangers: One of the best ways to protect yourself from online predators is to avoid interactions with strangers online. This means not accepting friend requests or following requests from people you don't know, and not engaging in conversations with people you haven't met in person.

Keep your social media profiles private: Setting your social media profiles to private can help protect you from online predators. This way, only people you know and trust will be able to see your posts and interact with you.

Never share explicit photos or videos: Online predators may use explicit photos or videos as a way to blackmail or manipulate you. Never share explicit photos or videos of yourself online, even if you trust the person you're sharing them with.

Report any suspicious activity: If you ever feel uncomfortable or unsafe online, report the activity to a trusted adult or authority figure. This includes any messages or interactions with strangers that make you feel uneasy.

Be cautious about meeting people in person: If someone you meet online wants to meet in person, be cautious and always meet in a public place. It's a good idea to bring a friend or family member with you, and to let someone else know where you'll be and when you'll be back.

Keep your computer and mobile devices updated: Keeping your computer and mobile devices updated with the latest security software and patches can help protect you from online threats, including online predators.

Trust your instincts: If something feels off or uncomfortable in an online interaction, trust your instincts and end the conversation. It's better to be safe than sorry.

ONLINE SCAMS

As someone active on different online platforms, it's important to be aware of the many online scams that exist today. Online scams can take many forms, from phishing scams to identity theft, and they can cause serious harm to both your finances and your personal information. In this section, you'll find an overview of some of the most common online scams, as well as tips for recognizing and avoiding them (Pearl 2022).

Phishing scams: These kinds of scams are one of the most common online scams. They involve an attacker sending you an email or message that appears to be from a legitimate source, such as your bank or an online retailer. The message may ask you to click on a link or enter your personal information, such as your username and password.

To avoid falling victim to a phishing scam, you should always be cautious when opening emails or messages from unknown senders. If an email or message seems suspicious, don't click on any links or enter any personal information. Instead, contact the company directly to verify the authenticity of the message.

Identity theft: This is another common online scam that involves an attacker stealing your personal information, such as your name, address, and social security number, and using it to open credit card accounts or take out loans in your name.

To avoid identity theft, you should always be cautious when sharing your personal information online. Only provide personal information to trusted sources, such as reputable websites or companies. You should also monitor your credit reports regularly to check for any unauthorized activity.

Online shopping scams: Online shopping scams are another common type of online scam. They involve an attacker setting up a fake online store that appears to sell popular products at a steep discount. When you make a purchase, the attacker may take your money without sending you the product, or they may send you a counterfeit or defective product.

To avoid falling victim to an online shopping scam, you should always be cautious when making purchases online. Only shop from reputable websites and retailers, and be wary of any deals that seem too good to be true.

Social media scams: These scams are becoming increasingly common. They involve an attacker creating a fake social media profile and using it to scam users into providing personal information or sending money. For example, an attacker may create a fake profile of a celebrity and use it to ask for donations to a fake charity.

To avoid falling victim to a social media scam, you should always be cautious when interacting with people online. Only connect with people you know in real life, and be wary of any unsolicited messages or requests for personal information.

Tech support scams: Tech support scams involve an attacker claiming to be from a legitimate tech support company and offering to fix a problem with your computer or mobile device. The attacker may ask for remote access to your device or for payment to fix the issue. To avoid falling victim to a tech support scam, only trust tech support companies that you have researched and verified.

Employment scams: Employment scams involve an attacker posing as a legitimate employer and offering you a job. The attacker may ask for personal information, such as your social security number, or ask you to pay for training or equipment. To avoid falling victim to an employment scam, only apply for jobs from reputable companies and never provide personal information or payment without verifying the legitimacy of the employer.

Lottery scams: Lottery scams involve an attacker claiming that you have won a large sum of money in a lottery or sweepstakes. The attacker may ask for personal information or payment to claim your prize. To avoid falling victim to a lottery scam, remember that you cannot win a lottery or sweepstakes that you did not enter.

Romance scams: Romance scams involve an attacker posing as a potential romantic partner and using emotional manipulation to convince you to send them money or personal information. To avoid falling victim to a romance scam, be cautious when communicating with people online and never send money or personal information to someone you have not met in person.

ONLINE GAMING SAFETY

If you are someone who enjoys gaming online, it is important to stay safe and protect yourself from potential dangers such as online scams, cyberbullying, and other threats. Here are some tips to help you stay safe while gaming online:

Be aware of in-game chat features: Many online games have chat features that allow players to communicate with each other. Be cautious when using these features, and remember that not everyone you encounter online will have good intentions. Avoid sharing personal information or engaging in inappropriate conversations.

Report cyberbullying: Cyberbullying can be a serious issue in online gaming communities. If you experience or witness cyberbullying, report it to the game's administrators or moderators.

Use privacy settings: Many online games have privacy settings that allow you to control who can see your profile and interact with you online. Use these settings to protect your privacy and control who can access your personal information.

Play with people you know: Playing with people you know in real life can be a great way to stay safe while gaming online. This allows you to avoid potentially dangerous or toxic players, and to have more control over who you interact with online.

YOUR ONLINE REPUTATION AND SAFE SOCIAL MEDIA USE

You're probably well aware of the importance of maintaining a good reputation among your peers. Did you know that your online reputation is just as important? In today's digital age, your online presence can have a significant impact on your future opportunities, including job prospects and college admissions.

So, here are some tips to help you maintain a positive online reputation and stay safe on social media (Pearl 2022):

Think before you post: When you're scrolling through your feed and see something funny or interesting, it's easy to hit the "post" button without a second thought. Before you share something, ask yourself if it's something you would be proud to show your parents, grandparents, or even your future boss. If not, it's best to keep it to yourself. You don't want to share something that could hurt your reputation or be misinterpreted in a negative way.

Don't engage in cyberbullying: Cyberbullying is a serious issue that can have a negative impact on both the victim and the perpetrator. Never engage in cyberbullying, even if you think it's harmless. Remember, your online behavior reflects who you are as a person.

Check your privacy settings: Most social media platforms have privacy settings that allow you to control who can see your posts and personal information. Make sure you take the time to review and adjust these settings to your comfort level. This way, you can make sure only your friends and family can see what you post.

Avoid oversharing: It's natural to want to share every aspect of your life with your friends, but be cautious about oversharing. Avoid sharing personal information like your current location or your daily plans, as this could put you in danger. You don't want strangers to know your every move.

Be cautious about accepting friend requests: It's always exciting to get a friend request from someone new, but it's important to be cautious. Before accepting a friend request, take a look at the person's profile and see if you have any mutual friends. If not, it's best to decline the request. You never know who could be behind that screen.

Report inappropriate behavior: If you see someone engaging in inappropriate behavior online, don't hesitate to report it to the appropriate authority. This includes cyberbullying, harassment, and inappropriate content. You have the power to help create a safe online environment.

Take breaks from social media: Social media can be addictive, and it's important to take breaks from it to avoid becoming dependent or addicted to social media. Set limits on your screen time and make sure you're still engaging in activities that make you happy in real life.

It's time to move on to talk about something that is super exciting for a lot of teens... Buying your first car! There's a lot that goes into financing, shopping, and deciding on the car you want. But worry not, the next chapter will go over all the essentials you need to know before getting started

CHAPTER 11
A GUIDE TO BUYING YOUR FIRST CAR

Are you ready to take the wheel and buy your first car? This is an exciting time, but it can also be overwhelming. That's why we've put together this guide to help you navigate the process from start to finish. We'll cover everything you need to know, from researching the right car for you to securing a car loan and maintaining your vehicle. We understand that buying a car can be a big financial commitment, so we want to make sure you're equipped with all the knowledge and tools you need to make a smart decision.

USED VERSUS NEW CARS

If you're looking to buy your first car, you may be wondering whether to buy used or new. This is one of the very first things you will need to consider before even taking the steps in the next section. Both options have their pros and cons, so it's important to weigh them carefully before making a decision.

First, let's talk about buying a used car. One of the biggest advantages of buying a used car is that it's usually more affordable than a new car. You can often find used cars that are only a few years old and have relatively low mileage, which can be a great option if you're on a tight budget or don't want to spend a lot of money on your first car. Another advantage of buying a used car is that you may be able to get a higher-end model or more features for your money.

However, there are also some potential drawbacks to buying a used car. First and foremost, you may not know the full history of the car, which could include previous accidents or maintenance issues. To avoid these issues, it's important to get a vehicle history report and have a mechanic inspect the car before making a purchase. Another potential downside to buying a used car is that it may not have the latest safety features or technology, which could be a concern if you're looking for a car with advanced safety features like collision warning, lane departure warning, or blind spot monitoring.

Now, let's talk about buying a new car. One of the biggest advantages of buying a new car is that you can get a car that's exactly the way you want it, with all the latest features and technology. You'll also have the peace of mind of knowing that you're the only owner and that the car has never been in an accident or had any major issues. Another advantage of buying a new car is that you may be able to take advantage of manufacturer incentives, such as cash back or low-interest financing.

However, buying a new car also comes with some potential downsides. First, new cars can be expensive, and you may need to take out a car loan or make a significant down payment. Additionally, new cars can depreciate in value quickly, meaning that the car will be worth less than what you paid for it as soon as you drive it off the lot. Finally, you may not be able to negotiate the price of a new car as easily as you could with a used car, which could make it more difficult to get a good deal.

In the end, the decision to buy a new or used car comes down to your personal preferences and budget. It's important to consider the pros and cons of each option and weigh them carefully before making a decision. Whether you choose a new or used car, be sure to take care of it with regular maintenance and upkeep to ensure it lasts for years to come.

STEPS AND TIPS FOR BUYING YOUR FIRST CAR

If you're looking to buy a car for the first time, it can be a daunting experience. Don't worry, we've got you covered with this step-by-step guide (Baxter Auto 2022):

Budgeting for a car

The first step in buying a car is figuring out how much you can afford to spend. This means taking into account the total cost of ownership, not just the sticker price. In addition to the purchase price of the car, you need to consider the cost of gas, insurance, maintenance, and repairs. It's important to create a budget that factors in all these costs and make sure you can afford the monthly payments on your car loan. You can explore financing options such as car loans, leasing, or financing through the dealership. Make sure you shop around for the best deal and calculate the monthly payment you can afford based on your budget.

Choosing the right car

Choosing the right car can be tricky, but it's important to find a car that fits your needs and lifestyle. Consider factors such as fuel efficiency, safety features, and maintenance costs. If you live in an area with harsh winters, you might want to consider a car with four-wheel drive. If you're more concerned with fuel economy, a smaller car might be a better choice. You should also think about the features you want, such as air conditioning, power windows, and a good sound system.

Negotiating the purchase

Once you've found a car you like and fits your budget, it's time to negotiate the purchase. Do some research to find out the market value of the car you want to buy. This will help you negotiate a fair price with the seller. Be prepared to walk away if the price is too high, and negotiate on other factors such as financing, trade-in value, or add-ons. Remember, you have the power to negotiate, so don't be afraid to use it!

Test driving

Before making a final decision on a car, you should always test drive it. Take the car for a spin on a variety of roads, including highways, back roads, and residential streets. Pay attention to how the car handles, such as the brakes, suspension, and steering. Make sure to try out all the features, such as air conditioning, radio, and power windows, to make sure they're in good working order. If you're not comfortable with the car, don't hesitate to look for another one.

Finalizing the purchase

Once you've negotiated a good price and are happy with the car after test driving it, it's time to finalize the purchase. Make sure you have all the necessary paperwork, such as the title, registration, and proof of insurance. Read over the contract carefully before you sign it and ask questions if anything is unclear. Don't forget to get a copy of the contract for your records.

TIPS FOR FINANCING YOUR FIRST CAR

Financing a car can be one of the most confusing parts of buying your first car. How do you get enough money? What's a car loan and how do you get one? In this section, we'll go over a few of the different ways you can financially buy your first car (Baxter Auto 2022).

Saving up

Your first option is simply saving up enough money to be able to afford a car. You will need to keep a couple things in mind when doing this, including:

- Create a Budget: The first step in saving up for a car is to create a budget. Determine how much money you can set aside each month for your car fund. Consider cutting back on expenses that are not essential, such as eating out or buying new clothes. By reducing your discretionary spending, you can free up more money to put toward your car savings.
- Determine how much you need to save and for how long: Once you have a budget, you need to determine how much you need to save and for how long. Research the cars you are interested in and estimate the total cost of ownership, including taxes, insurance, maintenance, and registration fees. Divide the total cost by the number of months you plan to save to get an idea of how much you need to save each month.
- Set up an automatic transfer: To make saving for a car easier, consider setting up an automatic transfer from your checking account to a separate savings account dedicated to your car fund. This will ensure that you are consistently saving money toward your goal.
- Compare interest rates: When choosing a savings account, compare interest rates to find one that offers the highest return on your money. This will help your savings grow faster and help you reach your goal sooner.

Apply for a car loan

Financing your car purchase through a car loan is a common and popular option. However, it's essential to research lenders and compare their interest rates, loan terms, and fees before taking out a loan. Start by looking online for lenders that offer car loans and checking with local banks and credit unions. You can apply for a loan online, over the phone, or in person. To qualify for a car loan, you'll typically need to provide proof of income and employment, as well as your credit score. Keep in mind that having a higher credit score can result in a lower interest rate and better loan terms.

When considering a car loan, the first step is to research potential lenders and compare their interest rates, loan terms, and fees. You can do this online, by phone, or by visiting a lender in person. Some popular options for car loans include banks, credit unions, and online lenders.

Once you have selected a lender, you will need to fill out an application. Be prepared to provide personal information such as your name, address, and social security number, as well as proof of income and employment. You will also need to provide information about the car you plan to purchase, such as the make, model, and year.

The lender will then review your application and credit history to determine whether to approve your loan and at what interest rate. If you have a higher credit score, you are more likely to receive a lower interest rate and better loan terms.

Before accepting a loan, be sure to carefully read the terms and conditions, including any fees or penalties for early repayment. It's also important to calculate the total cost of the loan, including interest and fees, to ensure that it fits within your budget.

Once you have accepted a loan, the lender will typically pay the car dealership directly. You will then be responsible for making regular payments on the loan over the term of the loan agreement.

Family loan

If you have a family member who is willing to lend you money for a car, it can be a great option as they may offer a lower interest rate or more flexible repayment terms than a traditional lender. Before accepting the loan, it's important to have an open and honest discussion with the family member about the loan terms, including the interest rate, repayment schedule, and any consequences for missed payments. Make sure you fully understand the terms before agreeing to anything.

To avoid any misunderstandings or conflicts down the road, it's recommended that you put the loan agreement in writing. This can be a simple document outlining the terms of the loan and signed by both parties. You can also consider using a loan agreement template, which can be found online, to ensure that all necessary details are included.

Once the loan agreement is in place, be sure to make payments on time and keep track of your progress. Treat the loan as you would any other loan and make it a priority to pay it off as soon as possible. Not only will this ensure a good relationship with your family member, but it will also help you establish good credit for the future.

A GUIDE TO CAR INSURANCE

Car insurance is necessary because it protects you financially in case you are involved in an accident or your car is damaged or stolen. Accidents can be expensive, and if you don't have insurance, you could be responsible for paying for the damages out of your own pocket. This can be especially difficult for teenagers who may not have a lot of savings or income.

Furthermore, car insurance is often required by law. In many states, it is illegal to drive without a minimum amount of insurance coverage. If you are caught driving without insurance, you could face fines, license suspension, and even legal trouble.

Let's jump right into everything you should know about car insurance (Baxter Auto 2022):

- Types of coverage: There are different types of car insurance coverage, including liability, collision, and comprehensive. Liability insurance covers damages and injuries you cause to others in an accident, while collision insurance covers damages to your car from a collision. Comprehensive insurance covers damages to your car caused by events other than collisions, such as theft, vandalism, or natural disasters.

- Minimum coverage: Each state has a minimum requirement for car insurance coverage. Be sure to check your state's requirements and get at least the minimum coverage. However, it's always recommended to get more coverage to be fully protected.
- Premiums: Premiums are the amount you pay for your car insurance coverage. The cost of your premiums depends on several factors, such as your age, driving history, type of car, and location. You can lower your premiums by having a good driving record, choosing a car with safety features, and taking advantage of discounts, such as multi-car, good student, or safe driver discounts.
- Deductibles: A deductible is the amount you pay out of pocket before your insurance kicks in. The higher your deductible, the lower your premiums. However, be sure to choose a deductible that you can afford to pay in case of an accident.
- Claims: If you get into an accident or need to make a claim, be sure to notify your insurance company as soon as possible. They will guide you through the claims process, which includes providing information about the accident and getting an estimate for the damages. It's important to be honest and accurate when providing information to your insurance company.
- Shop around: Don't settle for the first car insurance policy you come across. Shop around and compare different policies, coverage, and prices from different insurance companies. Be sure to read the policy details carefully and ask questions if you're unsure about anything.
- Keep your insurance up to date: Be sure to keep your car insurance policy up to date by renewing it on time and making changes if necessary, such as adding or removing a driver from your policy.

CAR MAINTENANCE AND A GUIDE TO BASIC REPAIRS

As a new car owner, you may encounter a few unexpected bumps in the road, such as a flat tire or dead battery. While it's always a good idea to take your car to a professional mechanic for major repairs, there are some basic car repairs that every car owner should know how to do. Here's an overview of some important car repairs you should be familiar with:

- Changing a flat tire: If you experience a flat tire while driving, you can change it yourself with a spare tire and a few basic tools. First, park your car on a flat, level surface and engage the parking brake. Then, use a lug wrench to loosen the lug nuts on the flat tire. Next, use a car jack to lift the car off the ground and remove the lug nuts and flat tire. Finally, place the spare tire on the car and tighten the lug nuts, being careful not to over-tighten them. It's important to note that spare tires are meant to be used temporarily and should not be driven at high speeds for long distances.

- Replacing the car battery: If your car battery dies, you can replace it yourself with a new battery and a few basic tools. First, locate the battery in your car's engine bay and remove the negative and positive cables from the old battery using a wrench. Be sure to remove the negative cable first (usually colored black) and then the positive cables (often in red). Next, remove the battery clamp or bracket that holds the battery in place. Then, remove the old battery and replace it with the new battery, making sure to reconnect the cables in the correct order. Finally, tighten the battery clamp or bracket to secure the new battery in place.

- Changing the oil: Oil changes are necessary to keep your car running smoothly. Check your car's manual to determine how often your car needs an oil change. Changing the oil is a simple process that involves draining the old oil, replacing the oil filter, and filling the engine with new oil.

- Replacing the brake pads: Brake pads wear out over time and need to be replaced to ensure safe driving. Signs that it's time to replace your brake pads include squeaking or grinding sounds when you brake. Replacing brake pads involves removing the wheel, removing the old brake pads, and installing new ones.

- Changing the spark plugs: Spark plugs ignite the fuel in your engine and need to be changed every 30,000 to 100,000 miles, depending on your car's make and model. Signs that your spark plugs need to be changed include difficulty starting your car and decreased fuel efficiency. Changing spark plugs involves removing the old plugs and installing new ones.

- Replacing the air filter: Air filters keep debris and dirt from entering your engine, and need to be replaced regularly to ensure optimal engine performance. Signs that your air filter needs to be replaced include reduced fuel efficiency and decreased engine power.

Replacing the air filter is a simple process that involves locating the air filter housing, removing the old filter, and installing a new one.

EMERGENCY PREPAREDNESS AND SAFE DRIVING

When you are first practicing driving and getting used to being behind the wheel, safe driving is key. Here are some tips to practice safe driving (Baxter Auto 2022):

- Avoid distractions: Distracted driving is a leading cause of accidents on the road. Avoid texting or using your phone while driving, as well as eating, drinking, or doing anything that takes your attention away from the road. If you need to use your phone, pull over to a safe location and park your car.
- Follow traffic laws: Traffic laws exist to keep you and other drivers safe on the road. Always obey traffic signs, speed limits, and traffic signals.
- Be aware of other drivers: Defensive driving is an essential skill for staying safe on the road. Always be aware of your surroundings and watch for other drivers' behavior. Keep an eye out for aggressive drivers, drivers who may be distracted or impaired, and other potential hazards on the road.
- Keep a safe following distance: Always maintain a safe distance between your car and the car in front of you. A good rule of thumb is to keep at least a 3-second following distance.
- Use turn signals: Always use your turn signals when changing lanes or making turns. This alerts other drivers of your intentions and helps to prevent accidents.
- Check your blind spots: Before changing lanes, make sure to check your blind spots by looking over your shoulder. This can help you avoid hitting another vehicle that may be in your blind spot.
- Obey speed limits: Follow the posted speed limits, especially in residential areas or school zones. Speeding can result in accidents and costly fines.
- Avoid aggressive driving: Avoid aggressive driving behaviors, such as tailgating, weaving in and out of traffic, or honking excessively. These behaviors can lead to accidents and road rage incidents.

As a new driver, it's also important to be prepared for emergencies on the road. Here are a few ways you can be prepared for anything (Baxter Auto 2022):

- Keep a spare tire and emergency kit in the car: A flat tire or a dead battery can happen unexpectedly, leaving you stranded on the road. Make sure you have a spare tire in good condition, along with the necessary tools to change it. It's also a good idea to keep an emergency kit in your car, which should include items such as jumper cables, flashlight, first-aid kit, reflective vest, and water and snacks.
- Regular maintenance: Preventive maintenance is crucial for ensuring your car is in good condition and reducing the risk of breakdowns. Regularly check your oil level, tire pressure, brakes, and other vital components of your car. If you notice any issues, get them fixed promptly to avoid potential problems on the road.
- Know how to handle emergencies: In case of an emergency, it's important to know how to react. If you're involved in an accident, stay calm, and assess the situation. If there are injuries or damage, call emergency services right away. If your car breaks down or you get a flat tire, move your vehicle to a safe location, away from traffic, and use your hazard lights to warn other drivers. Be prepared to call for help if needed.

A GUIDE TO CAR MODIFICATIONS

As a new car owner and driver, you may be starting to think about customizing your car to make it stand out from the crowd. While car modifications can be a fun and exciting way to express yourself and make your vehicle unique, it's essential to choose modifications that are safe and legal. In this section, we'll provide you with an introduction to car modifications, and some tips for choosing modifications that will keep you and your passengers safe on the road.

Car modifications refer to any changes or alterations made to a vehicle to improve its performance, appearance, or functionality. This can include upgrading the engine, suspension, brakes, exhaust, and other mechanical components. It can also include aesthetic changes such as adding body kits, spoilers, and new wheels. In addition to these modifications, many car owners also like to add accessories to their vehicles, such as bike racks, cargo carriers, and sound systems.

There are many reasons why you might consider modifying your car. For some people, it's a way to improve the performance of the vehicle, making it faster, more agile, or more powerful. For others, it's a way to make the car look more stylish or unique. And for some, it's about creating a more comfortable or convenient driving experience.

However, it's key to note that not all car modifications are made equal. Some modifications can actually decrease the safety of your vehicle or even make it illegal to drive on public roads. That's why it's crucial to choose your modifications carefully.

Here are some tips for choosing car modifications that are safe and legal:

Check the laws in your area: Laws and regulations regarding car modifications can vary widely depending on where you live. Before you start making any changes to your vehicle, make sure you research the laws in your area to find out what modifications are legal and what modifications are not.

Stick to reputable brands: When choosing modifications for your car, it's important to stick to brands that have a good reputation for quality and safety. Avoid cheap, no-name brands that may not meet safety standards, or may not be backed by a warranty.

Consider the impact on safety: Before making any modifications to your car, consider how they will impact the safety of the vehicle. Will they decrease handling, braking, or stability? Will they make it harder for you to see out of the vehicle or to communicate with other drivers?

Let's go over some of the different modifications you might be considering and how you can go about them in responsible ways (Dallman 2019):

Upgrading your sound system: One popular modification that many teens consider is upgrading their car's sound system. While a great sound system can enhance your driving experience and make listening to music more enjoyable, just make sure your new sound system is installed safely and securely. The last thing you want is for your speakers to come loose and cause a distraction while you're driving. While it's tempting to turn up the volume and blast your favorite tunes, it's essential to remember that excessively loud music can be dangerous and distracting. Keep the volume at a reasonable level so you can still hear emergency vehicles, honking horns, and other important sounds on the road.

Keep in mind that laws regarding sound systems can vary by state and locality. Some areas have limits on the volume of music that can be played while driving, so be sure to check your local laws before making any modifications.

Wheel and tire upgrades: Upgrading your wheels and tires can improve the performance and appearance of your car. However, it's crucial to choose a size and offset that is compatible with your car's suspension and won't cause rubbing or clearance issues. It's also essential to choose high-quality tires that are appropriate for your driving conditions.

Body kits and aero upgrades: Adding a body kit or aerodynamic upgrades can improve the appearance and performance of your car.

Adding Accessories: Adding accessories to your car can also be a fun way to customize your vehicle. Be sure to choose accessories that won't obstruct your view: Accessories such as bike racks or cargo carriers can be helpful, but make sure they don't block your line of sight while driving. You need to be able to see clearly out of your windows and mirrors to avoid accidents. Also always make sure to secure them and consider the weight of the accessories and how they might affect your car.

Interior upgrades: Upgrading your car's interior can improve comfort and add a more customized look. It is essential to choose modifications that won't interfere with the functionality of your car's controls or airbags. It's also important to choose materials that are safe and won't release harmful chemicals or fumes.

Cooling upgrades: If you're interested in high-performance driving, upgrading your car's cooling system can help prevent overheating and improve performance. However, it's important to choose a reputable brand and ensure that the upgrades are installed correctly to avoid compromising the safety and reliability of your car.

Bracing and reinforcement: Adding braces or reinforcement can improve the rigidity and handling of your car. Just be sure to choose a reputable brand and ensure that the modifications are installed correctly to avoid compromising the safety and structural integrity of your car.

In the upcoming chapter you will discover another guide to a part of life that may seem quite daunting... pursuing careers and passions. How do you choose a path? Do you follow what you are passionate about? These questions will all be answered in the coming pages!

CHAPTER 12
EXPLORING POTENTIAL CAREERS AND PURSUING PASSIONS

You may already be feeling pressure from your parents or teachers to start thinking about your future and what career path you want to pursue. It can be overwhelming to try to figure out what you want to do for the rest of your life, especially when you're still figuring out who you are and what you enjoy. However, it's important to remember that you don't have to figure everything out right now, and that it's okay to explore different interests and passions before committing to a specific career path. In this chapter, we'll explore strategies for identifying your passions and interests, and how to pursue potential career paths that align with your values and strengths. Whether you're interested in seeking out a traditional job or want to pursue an unconventional path, this chapter will provide you with the tools and resources you need to start exploring your options and following your dreams.

A GUIDE TO IDENTIFYING YOUR INTERESTS

If you're unsure about what interests you and what you're passionate about, it can be challenging to determine your future. However, there are several strategies you can use to identify your interests, including exploring hobbies and extracurricular activities. Here are some tips to help you get started:

Make a list of your favorite hobbies and activities: Start by writing down all the things you enjoy doing in your free time. This could be anything from sports to reading books to playing video games. Once you have a list, think about what it is that you enjoy about each activity. Is it the social aspect, the physical challenge, or the mental stimulation?

Try new things: If you're not sure what you enjoy doing, try new things! Join a club or organization at your school or in your community, take a class, or volunteer for a cause you're interested in. Trying new things is a great way to discover new interests and passions.

Follow your curiosity and consider your values: Pay attention to what topics or issues you find yourself naturally drawn to. This could be anything from science and technology to social justice and activism. Following your curiosity can guide you to your passions and potential career paths. Think about what values are important to you, such as environmental sustainability or social justice. Identifying your values can help determine what career paths and activities align with your beliefs.

Use social media: Social media can be a great tool for exploring your interests and passions. Follow influencers or organizations in fields that pique your interest to learn more about them. You can find people on places like Pinterest, Instagram, and Tik Tok. This is an easy way to discover new jobs that you may have never even heard of before

Talk to friends and family: Sometimes it's hard to see our own passions and interests, but others may be able to provide insight. Talk to your friends and family about what they think your strengths are and what they've noticed you enjoy doing.

Reflect on your experiences: Think about experiences that have made you feel fulfilled or energized. This could be anything from winning a sports game to volunteering at a local charity event. Reflecting on these experiences is a great way to identify what you're passionate about and what career paths might interest you.

RESEARCHING CAREERS

It's never too early to start exploring and researching potential careers, so you can make informed decisions about your education and future job opportunities. In this guide, we'll talk about why researching careers is important, what to research, and some tips and tricks to help you on your journey.

By learning about different career paths, you can find out which ones match your interests, skills, and values. This can help you choose the right courses to take in high school and college, and can also help you make informed decisions about internships and job shadowing opportunities.

Additionally, researching careers early on can help you avoid making hasty decisions that you may regret later. If you start researching careers now, you'll have plenty of time to explore your options and make informed decisions about your future.

When exploring different careers, there are several important things to research to help you make the right decisions about your future. Here are some ways to get ahead on career research (Alexander 2022):

Start early: The earlier you start researching careers, the more time you'll have to explore your options and make informed choices. Don't wait until the last minute to start thinking about your future!

Use online resources: There are plenty of online resources available to help you research different careers. Some good places to start include the Bureau of Labor Statistics website, which provides information about job outlook and salary data, and CareerOneStop.org, which offers career exploration tools and job search resources.

Talk to people in the field: If you know someone who works in a field you're interested in, ask them about their job and what they like and don't like about it. You can also reach out to professionals through LinkedIn or other networking sites.

Attend job fairs and career events: Job fairs and career events can be a great way to learn more about different careers and connect with professionals in the field. Look for events in your area and make a plan to attend.

Job shadow or intern: If you're really serious about a particular career, consider job shadowing or interning with a company in that field. This can give you valuable hands-on experience and help you decide if this career is right for you.

Keep an open mind: Don't limit yourself to just one career path. It's important to keep an open mind and explore different options, even if they may not seem like an obvious fit at first. You never know what opportunities may come your way, and being open to different career paths can help you find your true passion.

Consider your strengths and interests: When researching careers, think about your strengths and interests. What do you enjoy doing? What are you good at? By focusing on careers that align with your values and talents, you'll be more likely to find a career that you'll enjoy and be successful in.

Talk to your guidance counselor: Your guidance counselor can be a valuable resource when researching careers. They can help you explore different options, provide guidance on course selection, and connect you with resources and professionals in your desired field.

Take career and personality assessment tests: There are several career assessment tests available online that can help you identify your strengths and interests, and suggest potential career paths. Some popular options include the Myers-Briggs Type Indicator and the Strong Interest Inventory.

Once you have found a career direction you want to follow you will need to start looking at specific companies and job possibilities. It's important to know what the day-to-day tasks of a job will be to determine if it's a good fit for you. For example, if you're considering a career as a nurse, you'll want to know if you'll be working directly with patients, administering medication, and monitoring vital signs, or if you'll have other responsibilities like managing and organizing patient records for the hospital.

Understanding the earning potential of a job is another important factor to consider when choosing a career. Researching the salary range for different positions can help you determine if a career will provide the financial stability you need. It's also important to consider factors that can affect your salary, such as experience, education, or location. For example, a software developer in San Francisco will likely earn a higher salary than a developer in a smaller city.

Knowing what education or training is required for a job is also necessary in order to determine if you have the qualifications needed to pursue a certain career. Researching what degrees or certifications are required can also help you plan the time and financial commitment necessary to obtain the required qualifications. For example, a career in healthcare may require a bachelor's degree in nursing or a specific certification.

The job outlook for a career can further help you determine if it's a growing field with plenty of opportunities or a declining field with limited prospects. For example, careers in technology and healthcare are currently experiencing growth and are projected to continue to grow in the future.

Lastly, knowing what the work environment will be like is important to determine if a career will fit your lifestyle and preferences. For example, if you prefer working outdoors, a career in forestry or landscaping may be a good fit for you, while a career in finance or accounting may require you to spend more time indoors.

QUESTIONS AND PROMPTS FOR CAREER AND HIGHER EDUCATION EXPLORATION

It's time to get down to business and organize your thoughts. You might have no idea where to start in your future career and higher education, so this list of prompts and questions will help you to gain some clarity.

- What are some of your favorite subjects in school? How could you use these interests to guide your future career choices?
- Do you have any role models who work in a field you're interested in? What have you learned from their experiences?
- What are some career paths that you've never considered before? Do some research and write about what you discover.
- What are your strengths and weaknesses? How could you use your strengths to pursue a fulfilling career? How could you work on improving your weaknesses?
- Are there any careers that you feel passionate about? What excites you about these fields?
- What are your top priorities in a career? Do you value job security, flexibility, creativity, or something else?
- What are some career paths that align with your personal values and beliefs? How could you find work that makes a positive impact on society?
- Are there any extracurricular activities or hobbies that could translate into a career? For example, if you love playing video games, you could consider a career in game design or esports.
- Do you have any fears or doubts about pursuing a certain career path? Write about these concerns and explore ways to address them.

- What are some of the most important skills you'll need to succeed in your chosen career? How could you start building these skills now?
- Are there any internship or job shadowing opportunities that interest you? Write about how you could take advantage of these experiences to learn more about potential careers.
- What are some ways to finance higher education? Write about the options available to you and the pros and cons of each.
- Have you considered studying abroad for higher education? How could this experience benefit your future career prospects?
- What are some of your long-term career goals? Write about the steps you'll need to take to achieve them and the challenges you might face along the way.

DEVELOPING TRANSFERABLE SKILLS

As a teenager, you may not know what career path you want to take in the future. However, developing transferable skills can help you succeed in any career you choose. Transferable skills are skills that can be used in different jobs and industries. Here are some transferable skills that you can develop:

Communication skills: Being able to effectively communicate with clients and coworkers is essential for any job. You can develop these skills by participating in group discussions, taking public speaking classes, or joining a debate team.

Leadership skills: By learning to be a leader, you can stand out from the crowd in interviews and as an employee. You can develop leadership skills by taking on leadership roles in school clubs or sports teams, or by volunteering to lead a project.

Teamwork skills: In most careers, you will need to be able to handle working with a team and detailing with different voices. You can develop teamwork skills by participating in group projects or joining a sports team.

Problem-solving skills: Not everything will go perfectly during your work day, and learning to solve problems effectively will help you out a lot. You can develop problem-solving skills by taking on challenging projects or working on puzzles and games.

Time management skills: Being able to manage your time and get everything done when it needs to be will be very helpful in any career you choose to pursue. You can develop time management skills by setting goals and deadlines for yourself, using a planner or calendar, or taking on multiple tasks and learning to prioritize.

Critical thinking skills: Critical thinking is the ability to analyze information and make informed decisions. You can develop this skill by asking questions, evaluating sources of information, and considering different perspectives.

WHAT IS NETWORKING?

Networking is the act of making connections with people in your industry or field of interest. These people can include professionals, mentors, teachers, or even friends and family. By building relationships with these individuals, you can gain insight into your desired field and even create opportunities for yourself in the future.

Networking can seem like a daunting task, but it's an essential part of building your future career. It's all about connecting with people who can help you learn more about your interests and eventually lead you to potential job opportunities. In this section, you'll discover what networking looks like, why it's important, and how to do it as a teen and as an adult.

Networking allows you to gain a better understanding of the industry you're interested in. By talking to people who are already working in that field, you can learn about the skills and experiences needed to succeed. Second, it can help you find job opportunities that may not be advertised publicly. Sometimes, jobs are filled by word of mouth or personal recommendations, and if you have a strong network, you'll be more likely to hear about these opportunities. Finally, networking can lead to lifelong relationships with people who can offer advice and support throughout your career.

Starting early with networking can give you a great head start in your future career. Joining clubs or organizations related to your interests is an awesome way to start. By doing so, you can meet people who share your passions and may have connections in your desired field. For example, if you're interested in journalism, joining the school newspaper club or the local journalism association can help you meet like-minded individuals and build a network of contacts.

Attending networking events in your community or job fairs is another excellent way to start networking as a teen. Although these events are often designed for professionals, teens are welcome to attend as well. By attending such events, you can gain insight into various industries, learn about job openings, and meet people who can give you advice and recommendations. Make sure to bring a few copies of your resume and business cards with you, so you're prepared to network.

Volunteering for events or organizations in your community not only helps you give back to the community, but it also provides an opportunity to meet people from diverse backgrounds. For example, if you're interested in pursuing a career in healthcare, volunteering at a hospital or a local clinic can help you gain experience, make connections, and learn more about the industry. You never know who you might meet while volunteering, so make sure to be friendly and introduce yourself to others.

Informational interviews are another effective way to network as a teen. You can reach out to professionals in your field of interest and ask if they would be willing to meet with you for an informational interview. This is a chance for you to ask questions and learn more about the industry. It's important to approach this with a professional attitude and respect their time by being punctual and prepared with questions.

Networking as an adult can be quite different from networking as a teen. While the fundamentals remain the same, adults have more opportunities to network, and the stakes are often higher. You may attend industry conferences, professional organizations, and meetups. Additionally, social media platforms like LinkedIn make it easier than ever to connect with professionals in your industry. However, the basic principles of networking remain the same—be professional, courteous, and authentic, and always follow up with a thank you note or email. Remember, networking is about building relationships, so take the time to cultivate and nurture them.

ENTREPRENEURSHIP—IS IT AN OPTION?

Entrepreneurship is the process of creating, developing, and managing a business venture to make a profit. It involves identifying a problem or a need in the market and developing a product or service that solves that problem or meets that need.

Entrepreneurship can take many forms. Some entrepreneurs may start a small business or create an app or website, while others may invent a new product or service that fills a gap in the market. Entrepreneurs can work in a wide range of industries, from technology and finance to fashion and food.

Many people pursue entrepreneurship over going to university because they want to be their own boss and have more control over their career path. They may also feel that traditional education does not align with their goals or interests. While a college degree can be helpful, it is not always necessary for starting a successful business.

If you're interested in entrepreneurship, there are several things you can do to get started. Here are some tips to start pursuing entrepreneurship as a teen:

Identify a problem or need in the market: Think about areas in your community or in society at large where there is a problem or a need that is not being met. This can be anything from a lack of healthy food options to a need for better transportation.

Develop a solution: Once you've identified a problem or need, start thinking about how you can solve it. Brainstorm ideas for a product or service that would address this problem.

Conduct market research: Before you invest time and money into your idea, it's important to determine if there is a market for it. Conduct research to see if there are other businesses offering similar products or services, and if there is a demand for what you're proposing.

Create a business plan: A business plan outlines your goals, strategies, and financial projections for your business. It's important to have a solid plan in place before you start investing time and money into your venture.

Get funding: Starting a business can be expensive, so you'll need to secure funding. This can come from personal savings, family and friends, or investors. You may also consider applying for grants or loans.

Build your team: As your business grows, you'll need to bring on employees or contractors to help you manage it. Start thinking about the skills and experience you'll need to make your business successful.

Launch and market your business: Once you have a solid plan and funding in place, it's time to launch your business. Start marketing your product or service to your target audience through social media, advertising, and other channels.

Starting a business as a teen can be challenging, but it can also be a rewarding and fulfilling experience. With hard work, dedication, and a solid plan, you can turn your entrepreneurial dreams into a reality.

But if you aren't super on board for starting your own business before graduation, entrepreneurship is always an option just after graduation or even after university! It's all about paving your own way and making the choices that suit your needs and goals.

As a teen, you may feel like you need to have your entire life planned out. You might feel pressure to choose a specific career path and stick to it for the rest of your life. However, it's important to remember that you don't have to do that. Many successful people have changed their careers multiple times throughout their lives. Take Dwayne Johnson for example (Pradeepa 2023):

Dwayne "The Rock" Johnson is a third example of someone who has pursued multiple careers and interests throughout his life. He started off as a professional wrestler and quickly became one of the most successful and popular wrestlers of all time. However, he eventually decided to pursue a career in acting and soon became a Hollywood star. In addition to acting, he has also started his own production company and has become a successful entrepreneur. The Rock is known for his hard work and dedication and has shown that with perseverance and determination, you can achieve anything you set your mind to.

The key to successfully changing careers is to stay open to new opportunities and to be willing to take risks. You can start exploring different career paths by taking courses or workshops in different fields, talking to people who work in those fields, or volunteering or interning in related organizations. By gaining new skills and experiences, you can develop a diverse set of abilities that will help you in whatever career path you choose.

Transitioning into adulthood can be intimidating, but by learning how to care for yourself, cook, grocery shop, and keep your space organized, you can make the change so much smoother!

CHAPTER 13
A GUIDE TO ESSENTIAL HOUSEHOLD SKILLS

As you grow older, you will soon come to realize that there are certain household skills that you will need to master in order to be self-sufficient and independent. While these skills may not seem important now, they will become increasingly valuable as you enter adulthood and start living on your own. In this chapter, we will explore some of the most essential household skills that every teenage boy should learn. From cooking and cleaning to shopping and making basic repairs, these skills will not only help you save money and time, but also boost your confidence and prepare you for a successful future. So, let's get started on your journey to becoming a capable and responsible young man.

COOKING BASICS

Being able to cook not only allows you to eat healthy and delicious meals, but also helps you save money and impress your friends and family. In this guide, we will teach you some basic kitchen skills and how to put together simple meals.

Start with the basics: Start with learning how to use a knife and how to properly measure ingredients. Knowing how to chop vegetables and slice meat is crucial for any recipe.

Follow recipes: Recipes will be your best friends in the kitchen, and following them closely will give you greater chances at making successful meals. They will help you understand how different ingredients work together and how cooking times can affect the taste and texture of the final product. You can find plenty of simple recipes online or in cookbooks specifically designed for beginners.

Build your kitchen tools: To start cooking, you'll need some basic kitchen tools such as a frying pan, saucepan, and baking sheet. You'll also need measuring cups and spoons, a mixing bowl, and some utensils like a spatula and whisk. As you progress, you can invest in more advanced kitchen tools, but these basics will get you started.

Plan your meals: Before you start cooking, plan out what you want to make for the week. This will help you avoid wasting ingredients and allow you to create a grocery list. You can start with simple meals like pasta dishes, stir-fries, or salads.

Practice makes perfect: Don't be discouraged if your first few attempts don't turn out perfect. Cooking takes practice, and the more you cook, the better you'll get. Ask for feedback from family or friends and keep experimenting with new recipes and flavors.

Learn from others: If you have a friend or family member who is a good cook, ask them for tips and advice. Watching cooking videos or attending cooking classes can also help you improve your skills.

Clean as you go: This means washing dishes and wiping down surfaces as you cook. It's much easier to clean as you go than to deal with a huge mess at the end.

Experiment with flavors: Once you're comfortable with basic recipes, try experimenting with different spices and flavors to create your own unique dishes. Adding herbs, spices, and other ingredients can completely transform a dish and make it your own.

Don't be afraid to make mistakes: Mistakes happen in the kitchen, and that's okay. Even experienced cooks burn things or over-season dishes. Learn from your mistakes and keep trying.

By following these tips, you'll be well on your way to becoming a confident cook. Enjoy the process, experiment with different flavors, and most importantly, have fun!

A GUIDE TO GROCERY SHOPPING

Grocery shopping involves not only creating a shopping list but also comparing prices and finding the best deals. In this guide, we will take you through the steps of grocery shopping so that you can become a pro at it.

Creating a shopping list: This will help you stay organized and prevent you from forgetting essential items. Start by checking your pantry, fridge, and freezer to see what you already have. This will help you avoid buying things you don't need. Then, plan your meals for the week and add any necessary ingredients to your list. Don't forget to add basics like bread, milk, eggs, fruits, and vegetables.

Comparing prices: Once you have your shopping list, it's time to head to the store. When you get there, take some time to compare prices. Look at the price per unit or ounce, which is often displayed on the price tag. This will help you determine the best deal. For example, buying a larger package of an item may seem more expensive, but it could be cheaper per unit or ounce than a smaller package.

Stick to the outer aisles: Typically, the perimeter of the store contains fresh produce, meat, and dairy products, while the inner aisles have processed and packaged foods. Shopping around the outer aisles can help you make healthier food choices.

Don't shop when you're hungry: When you're hungry, everything looks good, and you're more likely to make impulse purchases. Make sure you eat something before heading to the grocery store to avoid temptation.

Finding the best deals: To find the best deals, you can also check out the store's weekly ad or coupon book. Look for items on your shopping list that are on sale. You can also look for store-brand items, which are often cheaper than name-brand items. Be careful, though, as sometimes the store-brand items may not be of the same quality as the name-brand items.

CLEANING AND ORGANIZATIONAL SKILLS

Are you someone who's always on the go, with a busy schedule filled with school, sports, and other activities? It's easy to get caught up in the hustle and bustle of everyday life and forget about keeping your living space clean and organized. But did you know that having a clean and organized living space can actually make you more productive and reduce stress? Here are some basic cleaning tips and organization ideas that you can use to keep your room and living space in tip-top shape!

First off, let's talk about cleaning. The most important thing to remember is to keep up with it regularly. Don't let your dirty clothes pile up on the floor, and make sure to put things away after you use them. Start by making your bed every morning, which will instantly make your room look tidier. Then, take 5-10 minutes every day to do a quick sweep of your room and pick up anything that's out of place. This will prevent clutter from building up and save you time in the long run.

When it comes to more thorough cleaning, start by dusting all surfaces in your room with a microfiber cloth or duster. This will help keep dust and allergens at bay. Then, vacuum or sweep the floors and wipe down any mirrors or windows. Don't forget to clean your bathroom regularly too! A clean bathroom will not only look better but also prevent the spread of germs.

Now, let's move on to organization. The key to staying organized is to have a place for everything. Invest in some storage solutions like baskets, bins, and shelves to help you keep your things in order. For example, designate a specific spot for your backpack, shoes, and sports equipment. If you have a desk, keep it clean and tidy by using organizers for your school supplies and paperwork.

Finally, make sure to declutter regularly. Go through your things every few months and get rid of anything you don't use or need anymore. Donate old clothes, books, and toys to charity, and throw away anything that's broken or unusable. This will not only help you stay organized but also make you feel more refreshed and energized.

HOME REPAIRS

You might not have to worry about household repairs right now, but when you become an adult and move out on your own these skills will be highly important for you to learn. From fixing leaky faucets to changing air filters, here are some simple household maintenance tasks that you will need to become comfortable with when you move into your first place (Sustain Recovery 2022).

Don't you hate the sound of a leaky faucet when you're trying to sleep? The water keeps plink, plink, plinking into the sink until you want to scream. This is not only a nuisance, but it's also a waste of water and can lead to higher utility bills. The good news is that fixing a leaky faucet is usually a quick and easy task that you can do yourself. First, turn off the water supply to the faucet. Then, remove the handle and use a wrench to tighten the packing nut. If the faucet still leaks, you may need to replace the O-ring or washer inside the faucet. You can usually find replacement parts at your local hardware store.

Another important household maintenance task is changing air filters. The air filters in your home's heating and cooling system help keep the air clean and free of dust and other particles. Over time, the filters can become clogged and less effective, which can lead to poor air quality and higher energy bills. It's a good idea to check your air filters every month and replace them as needed. Most filters can be easily removed and replaced without the need for professional help.

Finally, make sure to keep an eye on your home's smoke detectors and carbon monoxide detectors. These devices can save your life in the event of a fire or gas leak. Test your detectors regularly to make sure they're working properly and replace the batteries as needed.

Learning basic household skills will help you thrive on your own as an adult and even gain more independence while you are still living with your family. In the next chapter we will dive into something you might not have thought to be a skill that would help you in life… giving back to your community and the planet. Let's jump right in!

CHAPTER 14
THE IMPORTANCE OF GIVING BACK

Have you ever thought about giving back to your community and the planet? While it may not be something you think about on a daily basis, giving back is an important way to make a positive impact on the world around you.

Giving back to the community is a great way of creating a place where everyone enjoys living. It creates a sense of unity and lets people know that you are there to support them. Even further, caring for the planet is just as essential because it helps create a more positive and sustainable future for everyone around you. By volunteering your time or resources to help others, you can make a difference in their lives.. You can help make your community a better place by cleaning up litter, volunteering at a local charity, or lending a hand at a local event. These small actions can have a big impact in the long run by making your community a cleaner, more supportive, and happier place to live.

Additionally, giving back can also help you grow as a person. When you volunteer or donate to a cause, you're learning new skills, making new friends, and gaining valuable experience. These experiences can help you develop empathy, communication skills, and leadership abilities that will serve you well throughout your life. This chapter will go over a few different and simple ways you can give back to the planet and your community.

ENVIRONMENTAL CARE

Do you want to make a positive impact on the environment? One way to give back to the planet is by practicing environmental care. By recycling, reducing waste, and reducing your carbon footprint you can help protect the earth for future generations. Here are some tips on how you can get started (Shwartz 2022):

Recycle: Recycling is a great way to reduce waste and conserve resources. Let's talk about a few ways to get started:

- Find out what materials your local recycling program accepts
- Rinse out containers and remove any food or debris before recycling them
- Flatten cardboard boxes to save space
- Recycle electronics, such as old phones or computers, at designated drop-off locations
- Purchase products made from recycled materials

Reduce waste: Reducing waste can help conserve resources and minimize the amount of trash that goes to landfills. Here are some ways you can reduce waste:

- Bring reusable bags to the grocery store
- Use a refillable water bottle instead of buying bottled water
- Bring your own containers when eating out to avoid using disposable containers
- Use a reusable straw instead of a plastic one
- Compost food scraps and yard waste
- Donate or sell items you no longer need instead of throwing them away

Reduce your carbon footprint: Your carbon footprint is the amount of greenhouse gasses that you produce through your daily activities, such as driving a car or using electricity. A couple more ways you can do this include:

- Walk, bike, or take public transportation instead of driving a car
- Turn off lights and electronics when you're not using them
- Use energy-efficient light bulbs and appliances

- Choose foods with a lower carbon footprint, such as plant-based foods
- Plant trees and support reforestation efforts

By practicing environmental care, you can give back to the planet and help protect it for future generations. These small actions can have a big impact over time, so why not start making a difference today?

VOLUNTEER WORK

If you're looking for a way to make a difference in your community, volunteering is a great way to do it. Not only does it allow you to help others, but it can also help you learn new skills, make new friends, and gain valuable experience.

There are many different organizations and causes that need volunteers to help them carry out their mission. You can start by looking to your local schools and churches, as many of them have volunteer programs or events that you can participate in. This can be a great way to get involved in your community and meet new people. Even more, local non-profit organizations, such as food banks, homeless shelters, or animal rescues, often need volunteers to help them carry out their mission. You can find these organizations by doing a quick online search or by asking friends and

Community centers and parks also often have volunteer opportunities, such as cleaning up litter or maintaining trails. You can contact your local community center or park to find out about volunteer opportunities in your area.

Once you've found a volunteer opportunity that interests you, it's important to take the right steps to get involved. You can start by contacting an organization or event coordinator to express your interest in volunteering. They may have specific requirements or guidelines for volunteers, such as age or availability, so it's important to ask questions and get all the information you need.

From there, many organizations will require you to attend an orientation or training session before you can start volunteering. This session will give you more information about the organization and its mission, as well as help you understand your role as a volunteer.

Once you've committed to volunteering, it's important to be reliable and show up on time for your volunteer shifts. Organizations depend on volunteers to help them carry out their mission, so it's important to be there when you're needed. And remember to never be afraid to ask how you can help or suggest new ideas. People are always looking for volunteers who are willing to take initiative and go above and beyond what's expected of them.

HELPING THE ELDERLY

Many seniors may feel lonely or isolated, and your time and assistance can make a big difference in their lives (Schwartz 2022). Visiting a nursing home can brighten up their day and show them that someone cares. You can spend time talking to residents, playing games, or even reading to them.

Many seniors may also have difficulty running errands or completing tasks such as grocery shopping or picking up prescriptions. You can offer to help them with these tasks, either by doing them for them or by accompanying them to the store. This can be a great way to provide much-needed assistance and social interaction.

Support senior centers: Senior centers are community hubs where seniors can socialize and participate in activities. You can volunteer at a senior center by assisting with events, serving meals, or even leading activities such as exercise classes or game nights.

DONATING TO CHARITY

Another way to get involved and give back as a teen is by donating to charities or organizing charity events. Here are some tips on how to make a difference with charity work (Schwartz 2022).

Start by researching and identifying causes and charities that align with your values. For example, if you are passionate about animal welfare, you can donate to organizations that help protect animals or support animal rescue efforts. If you care about social justice, you can donate to organizations that fight for human rights and equality. Remember to check the legitimacy of the charity before donating.

Organizing a charity event can be a great way to raise awareness and funds for a cause you care about. Start by identifying the cause and deciding on the type of event you want to organize. For example, you can organize a charity walk or run, a bake sale, or a silent auction. Make sure to involve your community and spread the word through social media and local advertising.

Many organizations also accept donations of clothing, toys, and household items. Make sure to check what items are needed and ensure donated items are in good condition. In addition to donating money or items, you can also volunteer at charitable organizations. You can volunteer your time and skills to help with events, fundraising, or other tasks.

PARTICIPATING IN POLITICAL ACTION

While you might think that politics is only for adults, teens can play an important role in shaping their community and country. Here are some ways to make your voice heard.

The first step in participating in political action is to understand the issues. This means reading up on current events, policy proposals, and laws that may affect your community or the world at large. You can also talk to friends, family, or experts in the field to gain a better understanding of complex issues. By doing so, you will be better equipped to express your opinions and advocate for change.

Peaceful protests are a powerful way to make your voice heard and raise awareness about important issues. Before participating in a protest, do some research to ensure that the cause and organizers align with your values. You should also make sure the protest is peaceful and legal, and that you under-stand your rights as a protester. Keep in mind that protests can take many forms, including marches, sit-ins, or rallies.

Another way to make your voice heard is by writing letters to your represen-tatives. This can be an effective way to express your opinions and advocate for change on specific issues. You can write to your local, state, or national representatives, and you should be clear and concise in your message. You can also consider organizing a letter-writing campaign with your friends or classmates to amplify your voice.

Lobbying involves meeting with your representatives in person to advocate for change. This can be a great way to have a direct conversation and make your concerns heard. You can request a meeting with your representatives or attend a town hall meeting in your area. Before meeting with your representatives, be sure to research their positions on the issues and prepare a clear and concise message.

Remember that everyone's voice counts, and together, we can create a better world for ourselves and future generations. In the upcoming chapter you will discover more valuable skills that will help you throughout the rest of your life... personal safety skills. Let's dive right in!

CHAPTER 15
PERSONAL SAFETY SKILLS

It's important to learn how to protect yourself and stay safe in different situations. Whether you're walking home from school, out with friends, or exploring a new city, there are steps you can take to ensure your personal safety. In this chapter, we'll cover some essential personal safety skills that every teen boy should know, including situational awareness and first aid. By developing these skills and strategies, you'll be better equipped to handle potentially dangerous situations and stay safe in your daily life. So, let's get started and learn how to prioritize your personal safety.

STREET SMARTS

As a teenage boy, having street smarts can help keep you safe when walking alone or with a group. Here are some detailed tips and explanations to help you navigate the streets with confidence (Reynolds 2022):

Be aware of your surroundings: Always be aware of what's going on around you, even if you're walking with friends. Be mindful of your surroundings and keep your head up, paying attention to potential hazards such as uneven sidewalks, potholes, or broken glass. Also, avoid using your phone or listening to music when walking in unfamiliar areas, as it can make you less aware of what is going on around you.

Walk with confidence: When walking alone or in a group, walk with a purpose and maintain a strong posture. This can deter potential attackers and make you less of a target. If someone is staring at you or making you feel uncomfortable, look them in the eye and show confidence, as this can often scare them away.

Avoid dangerous areas: Stay away from poorly-lit areas, deserted alleyways, and places known for criminal activity. If you need to walk through these areas, do so quickly and confidently.

Trust your instincts: If you feel uneasy or sense danger, trust your gut and leave the area immediately. Don't second-guess yourself or ignore your intuition. Your instincts are a powerful tool that can keep you safe in potentially dangerous situations.

Stick with a group: Walking in a group can make you less of a target and provide safety in numbers. If you're walking alone, let someone know where you're going and what time you expect to be back.

Use self-defense tools: If you feel comfortable doing so, consider carrying a whistle, pepper spray, or other self-defense tool. Make sure you know how to use it properly and have it easily accessible. However, be mindful that these tools can also be turned against you if you're not careful.

Stay alert in traffic: When crossing the street, be sure to look both ways and follow traffic signals. Don't assume that cars will stop for you, even if you have the right of way. Also, be cautious when walking near parked cars, as someone could be lurking inside.

Be careful with strangers: Avoid talking to strangers who approach you on the street, especially if they seem suspicious or pushy. If someone asks you for directions or offers you a ride, politely decline and move on.

EMERGENCY PREPAREDNESS AND FIRST AID

Being prepared for emergencies and knowing basic first aid can help you stay safe and potentially save lives. Let's talk about how to become better prepared for emergency situations (Reynolds 2022).

Understanding what to do in the event of a natural disaster is crucial for staying safe and protecting yourself and your loved ones. Depending on where you live, you may be at risk from various natural disasters, such as fires, earthquakes, hurricanes, tornadoes, or floods. Each of these disasters requires different actions to ensure your safety, so it's important to be aware of the potential risks and how to respond.

One of the most important steps you can take to prepare for a natural disaster is to create an emergency kit. This kit should contain essential supplies such as non-perishable food, water, a flashlight, a radio, first aid supplies, and any necessary medications. You should also keep important documents, such as identification papers, insurance policies, and medical records, in a safe and easily accessible location. Make sure to regularly check and update your emergency kit, replacing any expired or damaged items.

Another essential aspect of natural disaster preparedness is knowing where to go if you need to evacuate. Familiarize yourself with your local evacuation routes and shelters, and make sure to have a plan in place for how you will get there in case of an emergency. If you have pets, make sure to include them in your evacuation plan and know where pet-friendly shelters are located.

In an emergency situation, every second counts, and calling for help can be the difference between life and death. Knowing how and when to call for emergency responders is essential, and can help ensure that professional medical help arrives quickly.

The first step in calling for emergency responders is to know the emergency phone number in your area. In the United States, this number is typically 911. Make sure to keep this number saved in your phone, and consider memorizing it in case you're in a situation where you don't have access to your phone. If you're in a situation where you need to call for emergency responders, the most important thing is to stay calm and provide clear, concise information about the situation. Be prepared to provide your location and any relevant details about the emergency, such as the nature of the injury or illness, the number of people involved, and any hazards or obstacles that might impede access to the scene.

If you're unable to make the call yourself, try to find someone who can. This could be a friend, family member, or even a passerby. In some situations, you may need to call for emergency responders on behalf of someone else, such as if they are unconscious or unable to speak. If this is the case, make sure to provide as much information as possible about the person's condition and location.

It's important to keep your phone charged and with you at all times, especially in emergency situations. Consider carrying a portable phone charger or keeping an extra charging cable with you to ensure that your phone is always powered up and ready to use. It's also key to note that in some emergency situations, such as a fire or gas leak, you may need to evacuate the area before calling for help. In these cases, make sure to follow evacuation procedures and get to a safe location before making the call. Remember that calling for emergency responders is not just limited to medical emergencies. If you witness a crime or suspect that someone is in danger, calling for help can also be the appropriate course of action. Always trust your instincts and err on the side of caution when it comes to calling for emergency responders.

BASIC FIRST AID SKILLS

Learning basic first aid skills is an essential part of emergency preparedness. Being able to provide immediate assistance to someone who is injured or in distress can make a significant difference in the outcome of an emergency situation. There are various ways to learn these skills, such as taking a first aid class or learning from reliable sources such as the Red Cross.

Some of the basic first aid skills you should learn include CPR, treating wounds, and stabilizing broken bones. These skills can be lifesaving in emergency situations and can help you remain calm and collected under pressure.

In addition to learning basic first aid skills, it's important to know how to treat specific injuries

Cuts and scrapes: Begin by washing your hands thoroughly with soap and water. Then, clean the wound with soap and water, and gently remove any dirt or debris. If the wound is bleeding, apply pressure with a clean cloth or bandage to stop the bleeding. Once the bleeding has stopped, apply an antibiotic ointment to the wound and cover it with a clean, sterile bandage (Pediatric Care Center, 2022).

Burns: Burns can be particularly painful and require immediate attention. If someone suffers a burn, the first step is to run cool (not cold) water over the affected area for at least 10 minutes. This helps to cool down the skin and reduce the risk of infection. While running cold water over it might feel good it actually slows the healing process and decreases blood flow to the area. Afterward, cover the burn with a sterile bandage to protect it from further damage and keep it clean. Seek medical attention if the burn is severe, or if you are unsure about the severity of the burn (Pediatric Care Center, 2022).

Sprains and strains: A sprain or strain can occur when a ligament or muscle is stretched or torn. The first step in treating a sprain or strain is to rest the affected area. Apply ice to the area for 15-20 minutes every 2-3 hours to help reduce swelling and pain. You can also take over-the-counter pain relievers like acetaminophen or ibuprofen to help relieve pain. Elevating the affected area above the level of your heart can also help reduce swelling (Pediatric Care Center, 2022).

Choking: Choking can be a life-threatening emergency, so it's important to act quickly. If someone is choking, encourage them to cough and ask if they can speak. If they cannot speak or cough, they may be experiencing a complete airway obstruction, which requires immediate intervention. Perform the Heimlich maneuver or abdominal thrusts by standing behind the person and wrapping your arms around their waist. Make a fist with one hand and place it just above the person's belly button. Grab the fist with your other hand and pull it sharply toward you, repeating this motion until the object is dislodged (Pediatric Care Center 2022).

By knowing how to treat these specific injuries, you can be better prepared to handle emergency situations and provide the necessary care until professional medical help arrives.

Life isn't always easy, and as you get ready to transition into adulthood you will be faced with harder situations. So, in the upcoming chapter, it's time to talk about how you can build resilience and overcome hardships.

CHAPTER 16

BUILDING RESILIENCE AND OVERCOMING HARDSHIPS

Life is full of challenges and hardships, and at some point, everyone will face adversity. For teen boys, navigating the difficult terrain of adolescence can be especially challenging. Whether it's struggling with school, coping with family issues, or dealing with personal setbacks, it can be tough to maintain a positive outlook and keep pushing forward. But developing resilience is key to overcoming life's challenges and bouncing back from difficult situations. In this chapter, we'll explore ways for teen boys to build resilience and overcome hardships. From developing a positive mindset to building a support network, we'll provide practical strategies for facing adversity head-on and coming out stronger on the other side.

WHAT IS RESILIENCE?

Resilience is the ability to bounce back from setbacks and challenges. It means having the mental toughness to face adversity head-on and not give up in the face of difficulty. Resilience is a crucial skill to develop because life is full of ups and downs, and everyone will face setbacks and hardships at some point.

Learning to be resilient means developing a growth mindset—the belief that you can improve your abilities through hard work and dedication. It means recognizing that setbacks and failures are a natural part of the learning process and that success often comes from persistence and perseverance.

Resilience also helps you manage stress and cope with difficult emotions. When you're resilient, you're better able to handle the ups and downs of life without becoming overwhelmed or giving up. You're better equipped to deal with difficult situations in a positive and constructive way, rather than falling into negative thought patterns or unhealthy coping mechanisms.

DEALING WITH FAILURE

The key is to learn from these failures and use them as stepping stones toward success.

One way to learn from failure is to reflect on what went wrong and identify the lessons that can be learned. Ask yourself questions such as: What could I have done differently? What did I learn from this experience? What can I do better next time? By reflecting on your failures, you can gain valuable insights that will help you avoid making the same mistakes in the future.

It's also important to surround yourself with supportive people who will encourage you and help you learn from your failures. Seek out mentors or role models who have experienced similar failures and have overcome them to achieve success. Share your experiences with trusted friends or family members who can offer constructive feedback and support.

Finally, don't be afraid to take risks and try new things. Failure is often a necessary step toward success, and you can't achieve great things without taking risks. Embrace the uncertainty and push yourself outside of your comfort zone.

A GUIDE TO POSITIVE THINKING

Having a positive attitude and mindset is essential for achieving success in life. Positive thinking helps you stay focused and motivated, even when faced with challenges and obstacles. It allows you to see opportunities where others see only problems.

When you believe in yourself and your abilities, you'll be more likely to take risks and pursue your goals. You'll be able to approach challenges with a can-do attitude, knowing that you have the skills and knowledge to overcome them. With positive thinking, you'll be more resilient and able to bounce back from setbacks.

Additionally, positive thinking can improve your overall well-being. It can reduce stress, anxiety, and depression, and promote better physical health. Research has shown that people who have a positive outlook on life tend to live longer, healthier, and more fulfilling lives (John Hopkins Medicine 2021).

One way to cultivate positive thinking is to reframe negative thoughts. Instead of focusing on what you can't do or what went wrong, try to focus on what you can do and what you can learn from the situation. For example, if you didn't do well on a test, instead of thinking "I'm stupid," reframe it to "I can learn from my mistakes and do better next time."

Another way to cultivate positive thinking is to practice gratitude. Take time each day to reflect on the things in your life that you are grateful for. This can help shift your focus from what you lack to what you have, and help you appreciate the good things in your life.

On the other hand, negative self-talk is a common experience, and it can be very harmful to your mental health and overall well-being. It can lead to feelings of low self-esteem, self-doubt, and hopelessness, which can hinder your ability to reach your goals. The first step toward overcoming negative self-talk is to recognize it when it occurs. This means paying attention to the thoughts and feelings that arise when you experience self-criticism and doubt.

Once you've identified your negative self-talk, it's important to reframe those thoughts in a more positive light. This involves challenging your negative beliefs and looking for evidence to support a more positive outlook. For example, if you catch yourself thinking "I'm not good enough," try to remember the times when you succeeded or made progress toward your goals. Remind yourself of your strengths and the things you're good at, and try to focus on these instead of your perceived weaknesses.

COPING WITH STRESS

Building resilience and mental strength will be key in learning how to handle stress. But in order to learn how to cope with your stress you need to understand where it comes from and how it could be affecting you.

When you're under a lot of stress, it can make you feel anxious, overwhelmed, and even depressed. It can also cause physical symptoms like headaches, muscle tension, and trouble sleeping (John Hopkins Medicine 2021).

One effective way to manage stress is through physical activity. Exercise can help reduce stress hormones in the body and release endorphins, which can improve your mood. Even just a 20-minute walk or run can make a difference.

Deep breathing and meditation are also great tools for managing stress. Taking deep breaths and focusing on your breathing can help calm your mind and reduce feelings of anxiety. Meditation can also help you develop a greater sense of mindfulness, which can improve your overall well-being (Lee 2022).

Talking to someone you trust about your stress can also be helpful. This could be a friend, family member, or therapist. Simply talking about what's causing your stress can help you gain perspective and develop strategies for coping.

Taking a break from what's causing your stress can be another powerful way to manage it. This could mean taking a mental health day from school or work, or simply taking some time to engage in a hobby or activity that brings you joy whether that's playing video games, listening to music, or spending time outdoors. Self-care is an important part of managing stress and main-taining good mental health.

Taking care of your physical health by eating well, getting enough sleep, and exercising regularly can help you feel more balanced and energized.

By learning how to cultivate a positive mindset, how to cope with stress, and create a healthy support system, you will be able to grow more resilient and overcome hardships. In the next, and final, chapter, we will talk all about how you can practice independence and become more responsible.

CHAPTER 17

TIPS TO GAIN MORE INDEPENDENCE AND RESPONSIBILITY

Your teen years will go by fast, and change will come quickly as well. One of the biggest shifts you will notice is an increasing amount of independence. With this newfound independence comes more responsibility. You may have more freedom to make your own choices, but those choices also have consequences. It's important to learn how to balance your freedom with wise choices, and make decisions that will help you achieve your goals and become the best version of yourself. In this chapter, we'll discuss the importance of gaining independence, as well as some tips on how to do so in a healthy and productive way.

SHOWING RESPONSIBILITY AT HOME

As a teen, you are likely eager to gain more independence and freedom. However, with independence comes responsibility, and it's important to show your parents that you are capable of being responsible and trustworthy.

One way to demonstrate responsibility is by taking on tasks and chores around the house without being asked. This can include things like cleaning your room, doing the dishes, or helping with laundry. By taking the initiative to complete these tasks on your own, you are showing your parents that you are responsible and capable of managing your own responsibilities.

Another way to show responsibility is by communicating with your parents openly and honestly. This means being honest about your plans, where you are going, who you are with, and when you will be back. It also means being responsive to their calls or messages while you are out. By keeping your parents informed you will prove that you are being trustworthy and responsible on your own accord.

It's also important to follow rules and guidelines set by your parents. This may include things like curfews, limits on phone or internet use, or restrictions on certain activities. Respecting your parents' rules, is also a great way of exhibiting that you are capable of making responsible decisions.

Finally, showing responsibility also means taking ownership of your mistakes and learning from them. If you make a mistake, be honest with your parents and take responsibility for your actions. Show them that you understand the consequences of your actions and are committed to making better choices in the future.

By demonstrating responsibility and trustworthiness, you can earn your parents' trust and gain more independence. While it may take time and effort to build this trust, the rewards of greater freedom and responsibility are worth it in the end. Remember to be patient, communicate openly, and show your parents that you are ready for more independence.

LEADERSHIP

Developing leadership skills and qualities can help you become more confident in your growing independence. As a teen, you have the potential to be a great leader. Being a leader is not just about having power or being in charge; it's about inspiring and guiding others to reach their full potential, both individually and as a group.

To be a great leader, there are several key traits you should cultivate. Firstly, communication is crucial. Great leaders are able to clearly articulate their ideas, listen to others, and give feedback in a constructive way. Good communication skills will enable you to express yourself effectively, build strong relationships, and avoid misunderstandings.

Leaders also have a clear vision of where they want to go and what they want to achieve. They are able to inspire others to follow their lead and work toward a common goal. You can develop your own vision by setting goals and working toward them, and by encouraging others to share your vision.

Empathy is another essential trait for any leader. A good leader is empathetic and able to understand the needs and feelings of those around them. This allows them to build strong relationships and create a positive team environment. You can practice empathy by actively listening to others, seeking to understand their perspective, and responding in a supportive and compassionate way.

Even further, leaders are confident in themselves and their abilities. They are able to make tough decisions and take risks when necessary. Developing self-confidence can take time and effort, but can be achieved through practicing positive self-talk, facing your fears, and seeking out new experiences.

Finally, accountability is a critical trait for any leader. Leaders hold themselves and others accountable for their actions and decisions. By taking responsibility for your own actions, you can build trust and credibility with others.

There are many ways you can work on developing your leadership skills. For example, you can seek out leadership opportunities at school or in your community, such as volunteering or taking on a leadership role in a club or organization. You can also read books and articles on leadership, attend workshops or seminars, or seek out a mentor who can provide guidance and support.

Remember, being a leader is not about being perfect, but about striving to improve and inspire others. With dedication and effort, you can cultivate the traits of a great leader and make a positive impact on those around you.

ACADEMIC RESPONSIBILITY

One of the most essential things you can do to ensure a bright future and a new level of independence is to prioritize your education and take responsibility for your own learning.

Education is the key to unlocking a world of opportunities, and setting academic goals is an important step toward achieving success. Whether you want to pursue higher education, enter a particular field, or simply achieve your personal best, setting clear goals can help you stay focused and motivated.

Once you have set your goals, it's essential to take responsibility for your own learning. This means being proactive in your education and seeking out resources and opportunities to help you succeed. For example, you can attend after-school study groups, seek out tutoring services, or work with your teachers to identify areas where you need extra support.

In addition to seeking out resources, it's also key to take ownership of your own learning by being an active participant in class. This means coming prepared to class, actively participating in discussions, asking questions, and taking notes. By engaging in your own learning, you will not only gain a deeper understanding of the material, but also demonstrate to your teachers and peers that you are committed to your education.

Another crucial aspect of taking responsibility for your own learning is developing good study habits. This can include things like setting aside dedicated time each day for homework and studying, breaking down assignments into manageable tasks, and avoiding distractions like social media or television while studying.

Remember, the decisions you make now about your education will have a significant impact on your future. By setting academic goals, taking responsibility for your own learning, and developing good study habits, you can lay the foundation for a successful and fulfilling future. So take advantage of the opportunities available to you, and remember that your education is one of the most important investments you can make in yourself.

CULTURAL LITERACY

By learning about different cultures, traditions, and histories, and cultivating respect for diversity and inclusivity, you can develop a better understanding of the world, what independence means, and who you are.

To begin developing your cultural literacy skills, start by taking the initiative to learn about different traditions, customs, and histories of different people and parts of the world. Reading books, watching documentaries, attending celebratory events, and traveling can all be great ways to start. You can also find online resources to learn about different people, histories, and places, such as online courses, blogs, and podcasts.

Avoid making assumptions or stereotypes about different people groups, as this can lead to misunderstandings and prejudices. Instead, see learning about different cultures as an opportunity to broaden your understanding of the world and appreciate the unique experiences and perspectives of others.

In addition to learning about different cultures, it is critical to cultivate respect for diversity and inclusivity. This means acknowledging and celebrating differences, and promoting a sense of belonging for everyone. One way to cultivate diversity is to actively seek out and engage with people from different backgrounds. This can be done through participating in multicultural clubs and events, attending cultural festivals, and making an effort to connect with people who have different perspectives and experiences than your own.

Another way to cultivate diversity is to practice inclusive behavior. This means treating everyone with respect and dignity, regardless of their background, gender, or identity. It means actively listening to others, being open to different perspectives, and avoiding harmful language or behaviors that can exclude or marginalize others.

FINAL WORDS

You are embarking on an exciting and challenging journey toward adulthood. Along the way, you will encounter a variety of situations and challenges that will require you to have a wide range of life skills. From developing healthy habits and managing your finances to building strong relationships and developing leadership qualities, the life skills you cultivate now will set the foundation for a successful and fulfilling life.

Remember that developing life skills is a process that takes time and effort, but it is well worth the investment. By taking the time to cultivate these essential skills, you will be better equipped to navigate life's challenges and seize opportunities as they arise.

Above all, always remember to stay true to yourself and your values. The path toward adulthood can be overwhelming, but with the right life skills and mindset, you can confidently face any obstacle that comes your way. So keep learning, growing, and striving toward your goals, and you will no doubt achieve great success in life.

———

Thanks for reading. If you enjoyed this book please consider leaving an honest review.

ALSO BY GRACE DANIELS

Life Skills for Kids

Life Skills for Teenage Girls

The Growth Mindset for Kids

The Growth Mindset for Teens

Career Planning for Teens

Social Skills for Teens

Building Confident, Brave and Beautiful Girls

Inspiring Stories for Confident, Brave and Beautiful Girls

Inspiring Stories for Kind, Confident and Brave Boys

BIBLIOGRAPHY

Alexander, Jamie. (2022). *Career exploration for teens*. NC State Extension Publications. Retrieved April 24, 2023, from https://content.ces.ncsu.edu/career-exploration-for-teens

Baxter Auto (2022). *Baxter Auto: Your guide to buying a car for the first time*. Retrieved April 22, 2023, from https://www.baxterauto.com/first-time-car-buyers/

Better Money Habits (2023, January 16). *Money management and budgeting tips for Teens*. Better Money Habits. Retrieved April 18, 2023, from https://bettermoneyhabits.bankofamerica.com/en/personal-banking/money-management-for-teens

Cedars-Sinai. (2019, February 13). *The science of kindness*. Cedars. Retrieved May 2, 2023, from https://www.cedars-sinai.org/blog/science-of-kindness.html

Dallman, Dean. (2019, October 22). *12 cheap car mods (with Price Estimates)*. Luna Window Tinting. Retrieved April 24, 2023, from https://www.lunawindowtinting.co.uk/cheap-car-mods-price-estimates/

Gordon, Sherri. (2020, June 11). *How to tell the difference between conflict and bullying*. Verywell Family. Retrieved April 14, 2023, from https://www.verywellfamily.com/conflict-and-bullying-difference-460495

Gordon, Sherri. (2021, July 26). *Everything your teen needs to know about setting boundaries*. Verywell Family. Retrieved April 19, 2023, from https://www.verywellfamily.com/boundaries-what-every-teen-needs-to-know-5119428

John Hopkins Medicine. (2021, November 1). *The power of positive thinking*. The Power of Positive Thinking | Johns Hopkins Medicine. Retrieved May 2, 2023, from https://www.hopkinsmedicine.org/health/wellness-and-prevention/the-power-of-positive-thinking

John Muir Health (2023). Nutrition for teens. Retrieved April 20, 2023, from https://www.johnmuirhealth.com/health-education/health-wellness/childrens-health/nutrition-teens.html

Lee, Erika. (2022, February 24). *Resilience: 5 ways to help children and Teens learn it*. Harvard Health. Retrieved April 27, 2023, from https://www.health.harvard.edu/blog/resilience-5-ways-to-help-children-and-teens-learn-it-202202242694

Luthi, Ben. (2020, November 18). *5 simple budgeting methods to help you live your best life*. LendingTree. Retrieved May 2, 2023, from https://www.lendingtree.com/student/simple-budget/

Lyness, D'Arcy. (Ed.). (2018, August). *How can I improve my self-esteem? (for teens) - nemours kidshealth*. KidsHealth. Retrieved May 2, 2023, from https://kidshealth.org/en/teens/self-esteem.html

Morin, Amanda. (2021, July 20). *7 ways to help teens and tweens gain self-awareness*. Understood. Retrieved April 13, 2023, from https://www.understood.org/en/articles/7-ways-to-help-teens-and-tweens-gain-self-awareness

Morin, Amanda. (2019, September 17). *Helping your teen with Time Management for a successful life*. Verywell Family. Retrieved April 20, 2023, from https://www.verywellfamily.com/teaching-time-management-skills-to-teens-2608794

Nikolopoulou, Kassiani. (2023, April 20). *Logical fallacies: Definition, types, list & examples*. Scribbr. Retrieved May 2, 2023, from https://www.scribbr.com/fallacies/logical-fallacy/

Old Mt Pleasant Dentistry (2020, May 30). *Hygiene for teens: Why good habits are important*. Old Mt Pleasant Dentistry. Retrieved April 20, 2023, from https://oldmtpleasantdentistry.com/hygiene-for-teens-why-good-habits-are-important/

Orchinik, Leah. (Ed.). (2023, March). *Dealing with bullying (for teens) - nemours kidshealth*. Kids-Health. Retrieved April 15, 2023, from https://kidshealth.org/en/teens/bullies.html

Pearl, Elana. (Ed.). (2022, August). *Online safety (for teens) - nemours kidshealth*. KidsHealth. Retrieved April 21, 2023, from https://kidshealth.org/en/teens/internet-safety.html

Pediatric Care Center. (2022, April 19). *Helping your child deal with minor illnesses or injuries*. Home - Pediatrician in Christiansted, St. Croix. Retrieved May 2, 2023, from https://www.pccvi.com/blog/554334-helping-your-child-deal-with-minor-illnesses-or-injuries

Pentis, Andrew, & Evans, Julie, R. (2021, August 15). *17 types of loans, from personal loans to mortgages and more*. LendingTree. Retrieved May 2, 2023, from https://www.lendingtree.com/personal/different-types-of-personal-loans/

Possing, Sandra. (2022, November 9). *How to develop Social Awareness: 12 steps (with examples)*. wikiHow. Retrieved May 2, 2023, from https://www.wikihow.com/Develop-Social-Awareness

Pradeepa, Sanju. (2023, February 23). *20 famous people with a growth mindset*. Believe In Mind. Retrieved April 18, 2023, from https://www.believeinmind.com/self-growth/famous-people-with-a-growth-mindset/

Reynolds, Nancy. (2022). *50 Potentially Life-Saving Safety Tips Every Teenager Should Know*. Raisingteenstoday.com. Retrieved April 27, 2023, from https://raisingteenstoday.com/safety-tips-every-teenager-should-know/

Raus, Emme. (2022, September 23). *How to improve social skills in teens*. Boys & Girls Clubs of America - Providing millions of kids and teens a safe place to develop essential skills, make lasting connections and have fun. Retrieved April 14, 2023, from https://www.bgca.org/news-stories/2022/September/how-to-improve-social-skills-in-teens

Schwartz, Marie. (2022, April 21). *50 community service ideas for Teen Volunteers*. TeenLife. Retrieved April 27, 2023, from https://www.teenlife.com/blog/50-community-service-ideas-teen-volunteers/

Sustain Recovery. (2022, August 29). *Teaching your teen important household skills*. Sustain Recovery - Adolescent Extended Care and Transitional Living. Retrieved April 27, 2023, from https://www.sustainrecovery.com/teaching-your-teen-important-household-skills/

The University of Queensland. (2023, January 23). *How to teach your teenager emotional intelligence*. Study. Retrieved April 13, 2023, from https://study.uq.edu.au/stories/how-teach-your-teenager-emotional-intelligence

Young, Karen. (2020, August 17). *19 practical, powerful ways to build social-emotional intelligence in kids & teens:* Hey Sigmund. Retrieved April 14, 2023, from https://www.heysigmund.com/social-emotional-intelligence/

Image Credit: Shutterstock.com